WOMEN WORLD LEADERS PRESENTS

VICTORIES

Claiming Freedom in Christ

VISIONARY AUTHORS
KIMBERLY ANN HOBBS & JULIE T. JENKINS

We raise a hallelujah to our Father God who has made this book possible through the power that works within each of us in an Ephesians 3:20 way.

Victories Contributors would like to extend a "very special thank you" to each of the following for their voluntary work of love, sacrificial giving and instrumental prayer support through the production of this book.

Kayla Follin

Barbara Wert

Shelly Haas

Kelly Hale

Lillian Cucuzza

Cindy Southworth

Michael Jenkins

Ken Hobbs

Women World Leaders Team of "Prayer Warriors."

TABLE OF CONTENTS

INTRODUCTION

You are about to dive into one of the most encouraging books you will ever read - filled with stories of women who have claimed victory in some of life's most difficult battles. As our enemy does his best to steal, kill, and destroy, the war he instigates rages on in lives around the world. But there is also an awakening and birthing of victory taking place in the lives of those who are Spirit-led and driven by God. This book has been written to proclaim these stories of God's overwhelming provision and care and share His Word with you and with the world.

It says in Revelation 12:11 that we overcome by the blood of the Lamb and the word of our testimony. We truly believe this scripture, and that is why we are led to share *Victories* with you today. As you read through these stories of victory and conquering the lies of the enemy, you will witness the power of Jesus to conquer sin and claim His goodness, His faithfulness, and shout His words boldly to all who will listen.

We are each a work in progress, trying to accomplish great and mighty things in our lifetime. Some of us may currently have challenges we need to overcome. Some may need to see a manifestation of God's power over circumstances in our lives. And others may be ready to proudly step forward and profoundly claim victory, sharing what God is doing within their own life. Wherever you may be on your journey, we pray this book will encourage and empower you to take hold of the victory that God has planned just for you.

We believe each person alive on this planet can be victorious in whatever situation life brings upon them by claiming freedom in Christ and following Him in active obedience, as God's Word tells us.

> But we thank God for giving us the victory as conquerors through our Lord Jesus, the Anointed One. (1 Corinthians 15:57 TPT)

We need not worry or be anxious in any of our trials or tragedies of life because God's Word is clear about victory in our situations.

> Yet even in the midst of all these things, we triumph over them all, for God has made us to be more than conquerors, and his demonstrated love is our glorious victory over EVERYTHING. (Romans 8:37 TPT)

As you read, get ready to be empowered to Claim your Freedom in Christ as you trust in His triumphant Victory for you!

KIMBERLY ANN HOBBS

As the Founder and Executive Director of Women World Leaders, a worldwide ministry that empowers women to find the purpose which God has just for them, Kimberly Ann Hobbs oversees all elements of the ministry, including *Voice of Truth* magazine. Kimberly is the co-CEO of World Publishing and Productions and an international best-selling author, speaker, motivational leader, and life coach.

As part of "Women World Leaders' Podcast," Kimberly hosts *Empowering Lives with Purpose* each week, interviewing beautiful women of various cultures from around the world. She shares written daily devotions for WWL on the private Facebook group and on the WWL website, www.womenworldleaders.com.

Kimberly has been a guest speaker on Moody Bible Radio Stations and made appearances on Daystar Television, sharing her passion for bringing women to a closer walk with Jesus through encouragement.

Kimberly is also an artist, with much of her work reaching around the world. She sits on the advisory board of Kerus Global Education, where she helps raise support for South Africa's orphaned children, whom she loves.

Kimberly is married to her husband Ken, and together they serve in missions and multiple ministries, and run their own financial coaching business. They have children and grandchildren whom they love very much and a home-life "Tiki Hut Ministry" in South Florida.

TURTLE FAITH

by Kimberly Ann Hobbs

> *Before you do anything, put your trust totally in God and not in yourself. Then every plan you make will succeed.* (Proverbs 16:3 TPT)

When God shows us a vision for something in our lives, He doesn't show us the entire plan all at once. Walking it out requires faith and can be like walking in the dark with a flashlight. We only see the ground in front of us illuminated, allowing us to take the next step forward. We can move and walk as long as we follow that light, which will help get us to our destination.

This is a great analogy to help us understand what a faith walk is like. Follow only the illuminated path that God sets before you, keep your eyes on Him and in His Word and proceed with trust as He guides, and you will be walking by faith.

> *But the lovers of God walk on the highway of light, and their way shines brighter and brighter until they bring forth the perfect day.* (Proverbs 4:18 NLT)

God reveals only what He deems necessary as we faithfully trust Him and walk forward. Receiving an unobstructed vision from God one day, I proceeded to cast this special vision that God gave me to the leaders at our monthly Women World Leaders meeting.

This vision was to have our very first women's conference, which would be a large event. Discussing this with immense joy and enthusiasm to the leadership team, the plan to execute was put in motion. We set out the very next month to make plans for the ten-month time of production ahead.

God told me this event would be big, and He gave me glimpses of all the work involved. The leaders were ready with great anticipation to see what was starting to unfold. God told me that women had been bound with hurts for years and needed the freedom this conference would bring. There would be guest speakers that would be invited to come from across the nation. We would have worship, prayer time, and an opportunity for some of our women to share their own victory stories in Jesus. God gave me the name to describe this future conference - The Soul Healing Summit. Everyone loved the name, and it made us even more thrilled to continue God's plan.

The leadership team began to form committees and gather volunteers. We set a date for the two-day event to be held in November, a couple of months short of a year away from the present time. We invited a sought-after keynote speaker and five other speakers, including myself, to highlight the event. We needed to fly four of the six speakers from other states, so we needed their verbal yes. We gathered for prayer weekly, and the leadership team and volunteers made grand preparations for this women's event. Nothing was to be overlooked because it was going to be a "conference of freedom" for every woman who came, and it would be executed with excellence for our Lord.

Step by step, God directed our path, and we followed Him. To raise the money to begin, we took an offering from our leaders. We secured a beautiful venue at one of the largest churches in the area. We knew God was leading. We booked the flights for all the guest speakers who gave their "yes" to be part of The Soul Healing Summit. We made extensive plans on how to market this event, making certain that women from everywhere would have the opportunity to attend if they desired. We made beautiful announcements and gorgeous colored invitations and sent them out everywhere. We put together advertisements for radio and social media. We were even asked to do guest appearances on talk shows to inform women of what this was about. We made beautifully filled purse-style canvas goodie bags for all attendees, put together with love. The stage was set with our steps ordered by God.

Months and months of escalating joy poured out of every leader and volunteer as they helped plan and prepare for this Summit. By faith, we stepped forward as God continued to open the doors. Money came in as tickets were purchased. We invested in banners and professional, heartfelt videos of some of our women sharing their stories. We produced a book that included many more women's stories of healing titled *Tears to Triumph*, which we would launch at the Summit.

God seemed to bring everything together on time as we inched closer, even selling out our VIP tickets. As the Summit drew nearer, confidence rose, and we were over-the-moon excited. Everything was in place! That is until... WHAM! The storm hit. And it almost stopped me dead in my tracks.

It was a bright sunshiny October afternoon as I sat at my dining room table with my partner in ministry, Julie. We were on her computer putting together the final speaking schedule for the approaching Soul Healing Summit when suddenly my phone rang. I paused, and although I didn't recognize the number, I sensed it was a local call, so I answered it.

It was a woman from the large church where we were to hold The Soul Healing Summit. She had sad news for me. "I'm sorry to inform you that you will not be able to have your event here," she said. SILENCE.

We had spent eight months tailoring the program to fit the layout of that specific church. This included multiple trips with the team planning stage preparations, lunch layout, and decoration placements. All the literature and invitations were printed and sent out. And instantaneously, everything came to a screeching halt. It was over just that fast. Just like that. No reason. No explanation. Just "We are sorry. So very sorry."

In that moment, I thought I was going to die. It did not compute in my brain. "What???" Speechless, staring out the window while Julie observed my face in utter shock, she overheard every word sitting inches away from me when the phone call came in. The tears began to flow almost immediately, until I was sobbing ugly tears into Julie's t-shirt as she pulled me closer to hold me tight. Everything - EVERYTHING we planned, all the work, all the money, nine months of preparation from the leaders and volunteers sadly vanished into an "I'm sorry" over the phone.

As I bellowed my deepest cries of despair, tears saturated Julie's t-shirt. I kept asking God in my head, "Why?" When my crying waned, we slowly sat back down at the table, just staring at one another. Her loving, watering eyes glared at me with concern. I still had not gained full composure. After moments of silence, Julie calmly voiced the question, "Do you believe God is leading us?" I continued focusing on her eyes, but no words came out. She proceeded to tell me that the way she saw it, I had three choices.

You can put this off until spring to give us ample time to find another venue. (We were only less than five weeks away at this point.) My answer was a quick no. The plane tickets were purchased and hotels booked for the speakers. It just couldn't be put off till April, I explained while wiping my wet face and blowing my plugged nose.

We could just cancel it all together since we have no place to hold it. "No," was the quick answer I replied again. The leaders and volunteers worked for months straight and were so excited. I knew tickets were sold already and the money had been spent in preparing. I couldn't even think to cancel.

Then Julie said, "Well, then your third choice is we trust God and continue with this speaking schedule we are working on and see what happens." Julie put her nose back into the computer and began to work again. I knew that number three was the choice, and without further hesitation, I slowly leaned in to finish our two-day itinerary. We worked hours, not discussing the fact we now had no venue for this massive event.

Still distraught after Julie left, I had my cry to God alone. I asked Him over and over, "Why? Did I do something wrong?" What seemed to be a door opened by God had just become frightful as it closed. Tables and chairs for the food to be catered in were reserved. The floor plan was laid out. This church venue provided so much. And the tickets were sold. Squirming doubts to all these questions kept pounding at my head. *What do we do now?* I felt the weight crushing me. Aimlessly I tried to answer my own questions, trying to find solutions as the week went forward, but to no avail. Stressed, my anxiety rose by the day. I felt responsible for all of it. And to top it off, my husband had booked us plane tickets that week to visit family. We had known everything was about finished so we could go away for a bit.

"How can this happen, God?"

Trust in the Lord completely and do not rely on your own opinions. With all your heart rely on Him to guide you, and He will lead you in every decision you make. (Proverbs 3:5-6 TPT)

Reluctantly, I left for our trip while feverishly making call after call to resolve a place to hold the event. Unable to rest while visiting family at home, I was in a tizzy. Seven days of what seemed to be dead-end calls occupied my time until we flew back to Florida.

Upon our return to Florida, my husband insisted we take a break. He felt I needed rest from the pressures and wanted to take me to the ocean. Complaining that I didn't have the time to spare, I ended up giving in, and we went.

We started out early that morning on jet skis, my husband on one and me on another. "Good," I thought, I would have time to talk to God alone on my ski, trolling down the tranquil intercoastal.

Not able to release the thought of the Summit, I knew in my heart to continue going directly to God for help. God had a plan, I just needed to talk to Him more.

As I set off on my jet ski through murky green waters inside the channels, I intentionally went slow, allowing myself the opportunity to pray. "God, I need to release finding a venue to You completely. It's killing me and I'm exhausted. I need to know that You will take care of it and this event will happen. God, I need a sign."

I had never asked God for a "sign" before this time. Did I really just ask for one? And what would this sign be? I had to make it something crazy difficult and almost next to impossible to happen, and if it came through, I would know 100% that God answered me.

In all my years of living in Florida and going out on the water, I had never seen a sea turtle in the wild. I knew they were rare, and this would be an outrageous request. Chances of this happening were slim to none. So, I prayed these words, "Lord, if you allow me to see a sea turtle today, I will know 100% that this is my confirmation from You that I can release finding a venue for The Soul Healing Summit completely to You. I won't stress another moment longer, nor doubt ever again that this Summit will take place. I will continue trusting by faith and believing the vision You gave me would happen, even without a venue. The turtle is my answer."

I truly had faith that God would show me a turtle, and it would be His yes to the Summit happening. I needed to hear from God, and He knew it. Scared and tired, I had done all I could do. I prayed just like I did other times, but now I asked specifically that a turtle would be my sign.

Enjoying our time on the skis, I stayed a distance behind my husband, slowly looking through the murky waters, putting along for hours. How would I even see anything in this water, I thought, let alone a sea turtle? Was I wrong to be intentionally asking God to show me such a far-fetched sign?

We decided to head out to the open waters of the ocean. The water was aqua blue and crystal clear. I was excited now... a chance to see my sea turtle. I had so much fun playing on the wide-open water, and time passed quickly. We needed to get the jet skis back by lunchtime, so we turned back to the water-way with no sign of a turtle anywhere. Then my jet ski broke, and I could only go five miles per hour. Ugh! I thought *this* might be my opportunity to look for my turtle, but there was still no sign. I trolled all the way back to the boat hands, who were waiting to put our jet skis up.

Ken had a boat planned for us for the afternoon. To me, more time to find my turtle. I told God as I jumped onto the boat, "I'm not giving up on hearing from You." Together, all 3 of us set out for the ocean once again - Ken, me, and God.

The day was beautiful. Kenny drove the boat, and I lounged in the sun. Exhausted and spent from the events of the entire past week and traveling too, all I wanted to do was focus on God speaking to me, my Rock, my Strength, and my Comforter. I never told Kenny of my request to God, seeing a turtle in the wild. I kept the significant meaning to myself, quietly nestled in my heart with hope.

Praise and worship music amplified as we traveled a mile or two along the flat ocean - no turtle anywhere. We anchored the boat near some rocks and listened to scripture reading, as Kenny and I love to do together when we relax. We munched on some snacks while anchored and gazed out into the pristine waters of the deep. A thunderstorm began to form, and we decided to pull up anchor and head back to the channel quickly. All day on the water I had prayed, talking to God, wondering if He heard me about the Soul Healing Summit. Would it ever happen, and if so, the bigger question was where?

Why didn't God allow me to see my turtle? Maybe it was my lack of faith. I don't know what the answer was at that moment, but I was sure glad that I had kept the request between God and me.

I knew at times that my faith may have staggered a bit throughout the day, but I held on to it and the request I needed from God. Oh, how I wanted to see a turtle! I knew God knew it too, my sign from Him that the event would be successful.

Then all of a sudden, out of nowhere, I heard Ken at the helm behind me, freaking out and screaming loudly while swerving the boat as if it were a car on a highway avoiding an accident. "Oh my gosh," he yelled.

I looked ahead, but there was absolutely nothing in my line of vision. Frantically I sat up from my reclining position shouting, "What? What is wrong with you? What is happening?"

I hoisted myself upward to look outward, but instead, I looked over the side of the boat. Out of nowhere emerged the largest sea turtle you could ever imagine - a "Goliath turtle!" It came up from the depths of the sea! Right beside me, on my side of the boat below my hand and arm, almost within touching distance, I saw him glistening out of the crystal-clear blue ocean water. With enough time for me to scream my head off, jump out of my seat, and look down at him in the water, he swam right next to me. It was a blip, not even seconds that passed, but I saw his large eyes as they glanced right into mine. A sight I will never forget as long as I live – ever! His eyes were fixed on mine. To me, it was like I just saw the face of God. Goosebumps galore, I knew it was Him.

Within seconds the turtle was gone - completely disappeared - never to be seen again. I could barely contain myself to tell Ken why I was so overly exasperated. Of course, he had no idea why I was going berserk. He didn't know that by showing me the turtle as His sign, God had fulfilled His promise to me, reassuring me that I could trust Him by faith and that I could know for certain that He would do what He said He would do.

Seeing that glorious creation from God confirmed to me that The Soul Healing Summit was in God's control, not mine. It reminded me that it would be Him, not me, that would bring this event to completion. I simply had to trust Him, get back to work, and continue doing what He called me to do – finish the mission. He would fulfill the vision.

You can process this story, understanding what God provided me that day on the ocean. God wants your plans to succeed too. He wants to provide for you too, but you are never meant to do it alone or carry the burdens when they get too heavy. Give them to God, completely. God wants your faithfulness to what He is calling you to do. He wants you to be successful. Please keep in mind that our successes differ from each other. Your victory story will be different than mine.

I didn't doubt a day further that The Soul Healing Summit would take place. I knew God had it taken care of that day. It may have looked a little differently than I originally thought, but that's OK. The Summit was God's success story.

We lost our first venue, but within days of seeing the turtle, God provided a better one. Dr. Art Keiser from Keiser University personally called me, saying he received my number from a friend who shared that Women World Leaders was in need of a location to hold a large women's conference. With tears in my eyes, I said, "Yes, Sir, we are." (And that's a whole other story...)

The Soul Healing Summit happened on the very same two days we had planned it ten months earlier. It was a 100% sold-out event at the Keiser University Palm Beach Campus Auditorium, with standing room only. The university not only donated the use of the venue, but they also provided personnel at their cost and exceptional food prepared on the premises. The list goes on of what God did on that faith walk. Souls were changed for Jesus. Women came forward for salvation, and God showed His faithfulness. Faith is the victory that overcame the shadows of doubt.

> *Now faith Is the substance of things hoped for the evidence of things not seen.* (Hebrews 11:1 KJV)

God revealed himself to me in a promise I asked Him for. Doing all the work He called me to do, I prayed without ceasing, and I was obedient to what He asked of me. I was faithful. Why wouldn't God have answered me? He moved on my faith.

What might it be that God is speaking to you, a vision, possibly a dream? Whatever He is revealing to you, remember to follow His lighted path. Walk close to God. Put aside what you may want for yourself to succeed and look to what God wants for you. You may not see the big picture right away, but pray and include God in your plans, because He knows the beginning to the end. Victory will be yours when you step forward by faith and take God's hand in yours. He will take the next step with you.

> *Commit your actions to the Lord, and your plans will succeed.* (Proverbs 16:3 NLT)

God is faithful to His Word and Jesus is faithful to forgive us even when we doubt or get discouraged. Are we faithful to what He is calling us to do? Victory is ours to claim. There is great freedom when we surrender everything to Jesus Christ and walk by faith, not by sight.

Conquering Fear

by Kimberly Ann Hobbs

There are two types of fear mentioned in the Bible. The first type is beneficial and encouraged, but the second type of fear is destructive to us as human beings and is something we should strive to overcome.

The first fear spoken of in the Bible is the fear of the Lord, which brings about many blessings and benefits, and is also the beginning of wisdom.

> *The fear of the Lord is the beginning of wisdom and the knowledge of the Holy One is understanding.* (Proverbs 9:10 NIV)

The other fear, the "spirit of fear," can come upon us at any given moment and is something we must learn to combat and overcome. It takes courage and strength from the Lord to conquer the spirit of fear. We need to trust in and love God completely to rise above this type of fear. God reminds us that as He cares for the birds of the air, so much more will He provide for His children.

> *So do not be afraid; you are worth more than many sparrows.* (Matthew 10:31 NIV)

Is fear holding you back from doing what God has called you to do? Please be strong and step out with courage. Why? Because God tells us not to be afraid of being alone or of being too weak, and He tells us not to be afraid to use our voice. God wants us to be heard. He also commands us not to be afraid of lacking physical necessities. He always equips us for the battle. There are admonishments throughout God's Word covering the different aspects of fear, including that we should not stifle our "calling in Christ" because of fear. I once heard a great explanation of this 4-letter word put into four simple words. Fear is: False Evidence Appearing Real. It's usually not a reality to what is happening but a mind alternative to what is taking place.

When we learn to counter the false evidence by putting our trust in God and then courageously walk forward by faith into the unknown, we will no longer be afraid of the things that linger or rise up against us. God takes our hand as we take our first step of faith forward toward victory.

> *Be strong and of good courage, do not fear nor be afraid of them; for the Lord your God, He is the One who goes with you. He will not leave you nor forsake you.* (Deuteronomy 3:6 NKJV)

JULIE T. JENKINS

is the Teaching and Curriculum Leader for Women World Leaders. Her duties include partnering with Kimberly Hobbs to run the ministry, writing for and leading the editing team of *Voice of Truth* magazine, and hosting 'Walking in the Word' - the biblical teaching arm of the *Women World Leaders' Podcast*. Julie also speaks at church events and retreats and serves as co-CEO and chief editor for *World Publishing and Productions* – a company that seeks to empower others to share their God stories with the world.

Born in Indiana and raised in Ohio, Julie earned her Bachelor of Communications at The University of Tulsa and her Master's of Biblical Exposition from Moody Bible College. She traveled with *Up With People*, was a long-time *Bible Study Fellowship* leader, and has completed multiple biblical and leadership training programs.

Julie and her husband Michael have been married for 25 years, live in Jupiter, Florida, and own and operate *J29 Marketing* – a full-service digital marketing company. They have three children of whom they are immensely proud.

Julie can be contacted at julie@womenworldleaders.com

THERE IS ALWAYS VICTORY IN OBEDIENCE

by Julie T. Jenkins

Have you ever heard God tell you to do something that, by worldly wisdom, made no sense?

I am a planner. I am not a risk-taker. So when God whispered in my heart to do something that was not in my plan, something that made no worldly sense, I wasn't sure that He totally understood my situation. But the lesson I learned in obedience, the victory He gave through the circumstance, was one I would come back to time and time again. What I learned was the essence of 2 Corinthians 9:6-15.

> *Here's my point. A stingy sower will reap a meager harvest, but the one who sows from a generous spirit will reap an abundant harvest.* (2 Corinthians 9:6 TPT)

After a job change in 2012, my husband and I moved our family of five back to Florida. My husband grew up in the panhandle of Florida, and we had spent nearly 13 years living in the Tampa area, so we were no strangers to the Sunshine State, but the West Palm Beach area was new to us. We were excited to come to a state that we considered "home" even though we were completely unfamiliar with South Florida.

We rented a small house near the beach – my motto has always been practicality, and if we can sprinkle in some fun along the way, that's a bonus. My husband and I both drove Hondas – I drove an Odyssey (a minivan), and my husband drove an Accord (a sedan). Not by design, they "matched" – both silver with the same grey interior. The minivan was long since paid off and was quite the mess, having been the taxi for three growing kids and two dogs for over a decade. The water bottles rolling around and the granola bars and tissues within arm's reach screamed, "I am a mom-van!" It regularly went into the shop, had taken us on many vacations, gone through a plethora of moves, and whisked us away from oncoming hurricanes more than once. But I was determined to drive it until the bitter end - until it wouldn't go anymore. And with this latest move, the miles piled on quickly. Each of our three kids attended different schools and the bus system was unreliable, so the mom-van worked overtime.

My husband's car, the twin, was quite classier. He was the businessman who took impeccable care of his car – keeping it spotlessly clean and ready to take a client to lunch at any moment. Although his car was also paid off, it was newer. As many do, he longed for a "better" car, but he generously and lovingly put his own wants and desires on hold as he provided the sole income for our family. With careful budgeting, his work had afforded us the opportunity to allow me to stay home with the kids, even if that meant that he drove a dependable sedan. Our "extra" money, for now, mainly went to kids' activities. God always provided for us financially, but the margin was thin – there was never a lot left at the end of the month. A fancy car would have to wait. And that was okay.

> *Let giving flow from your heart, not from a sense of religious duty. Let it spring up freely from the joy of given – all because God loves hilarious generosity!* (2 Corinthians 9:7 TPT)

As we got situated in our new home, our kids got involved in their activities. We had moved many times and learned that this was an essential part of their acclimation to a new community. We were thrilled when my oldest daughter landed a spot on a cheer team. Most teams have tryouts in the spring and then begin practicing over the summer for a fall season. The previous spring, she had trained for, tried out for, and become a member of a very reputable team – right before we found out we had to move. She was crushed. Not only did she have to give up her spot on that team, but we knew it was unlikely, given the timing, that she would be able to cheer that year in our new location. So we knew it was God's provision when we found out about a newly formed team. The timing was right, and Sarah made the team! The drive to practices was a bit cumbersome – about 30 minutes each way several times a week – but it was a sacrifice I was willing to make given the circumstances.

To my utter surprise, at the first practice, we found out that one of Sarah's new teammates lived within two blocks of us – and praised God that we could carpool. This was truly His plan!

Months went by. My husband got settled in his job, we found a church and Bible studies and got the kids settled into their schools and activities. The carpooling to cheer was going well – I took turns driving to practice with the other mom, whom I discovered was a single mom who worked several jobs to make ends meet. Despite her busy schedule, she always held up her end of the bargain and was as thankful as I was for the arrangement we had made.

In early December, after Sarah had been picked up to go to cheer, she called me and said, "Mom, we're stranded on the side of the road, and I'm not sure we are going to make it to practice." The car eventually started, and they did make it, but I offered to do the pickup that day.

The next week I called the other mom, I will call her Tracy, to arrange our driving schedule. In the process, I told her that I heard she had car trouble and I had no problem driving every day if she needed me to. She was SO thankful! She said that her car had completely given out. She gave me a glimpse into her life - telling me that a friend had been taking her to work, her daughter was riding the bus to school, and they were riding their bikes to the grocery store. She was upbeat and insisted that it would all work out, but yes, if I could drive that week, she would be grateful.

I got off the phone and realized how blessed I was – we had two cars that worked! I also thought about the fact that the only grocery store within biking distance from our little house near the beach was a very expensive one. The fact that Tracy and her daughter were being forced to shop at that store was surely an added financial burden on that small, resourceful family.

God kept putting them on my heart. The next week when I stopped to get gas, I bought a gift card from the gas station so Tracy could share it with the friend who was going out of his or her way to get this single mom to work. Then, when I stopped at the expensive grocery store out of convenience, the Holy Spirit dropped in my heart to purchase a store gift card for Tracy. I continued to drive every day to cheer. I put the gift cards in an envelope and wrote a card, "Tracy – I felt a nudge from the Holy Spirit to buy these for you. Please accept this gift that you don't need to thank me for and certainly don't need to repay. Consider it a gift from God. He loves you and is looking out after you and your daughter." I had NO idea if she was a Christian, or if she would think I was a crack-pot. I didn't care. As I dropped off her daughter, I handed her the card and asked her to give it to her mom.

Yes, God is more than ready to overwhelm you with every form of grace, so that you will have more than enough of everything – every moment and in every way. He will make you overflow with abundance in every good thing you do. (2 Corinthians 9:8 TPT)

By the time I got home, my phone was ringing, and when I picked up, Tracy was on the other end of the line crying. She opened up a bit, telling me how grateful she was for the reminder that God was taking care of her. She told me that she hoped to get a new car soon. I assured her that I could drive our carpool for as long as she needed.

But as the days went by, I could not stop thinking about their situation. I prayed and asked God what He wanted me to do, if there was a way He wanted me to help her. I was perplexed because I didn't know her well – we were like two co-workers who worked different shifts – we never even saw each other, but we both had the same job as a mom.

Remember my question at the beginning? Has God ever told you to do something that made no worldly sense?

Well, He did. God told me, as clearly as an alarm clock wakes you from a deep sleep in an otherwise quiet house, "Julie, I want you to give Tracy your husband's car." *What, God? You want me to give her the GOOD car? The car that my husband relies on to get to his job every day to earn a living for all of us? The car that he has taken care of and takes pride in? The car that we really can't afford to replace and that we desperately need?*

Now, I have to say, there aren't many times in my 25 years of marriage that I have not told my husband about something God told me – but there was no way I was going to tell him THIS! So I didn't. But I kept praying. And God kept saying the same thing. "I want you to give your husband's car to Tracy." *How do you even give someone a car,* I wondered? I Googled it. I made some phone calls. I got information. And I prayed. But I didn't tell my husband.

Then one night, my husband walked in the door from work, and we had the most unbelievable conversation.

My husband: "Did you drive Sarah to cheer today?"

Me: "Yes. Tracy's car is still not working."

My husband: "You know, I was thinking about that and praying about that, and you are going to think I am crazy – but I really feel like we are supposed to give her my car."

The world stopped. I took a deep breath and said: "Me, too. In fact, I Googled today how to give someone a car. But it makes no sense. That's our good car."

> *Just as the Scriptures say about the one who trusts in him: Because he has sown extravagantly and given to the poor, his kindness and generous deeds will never be forgotten.* (2 Corinthians 9:9 TPT)

Neither of us knew where to begin. Christmas was coming, and all the financial concerns that come with that holiday. We needed the car – but my husband actually had two weeks off coming up, we could certainly manage with one car during that time. And we didn't know Tracy that well – we definitely didn't want to offend her. These all felt like valid concerns. But God kept tugging at us.

So we made a plan – I told you I am all about plans! Even in our obedience, God works with our personalities! The plan was that we would continue to pray, and we would open up conversations with Tracy so we could discern if she would even want the car or if a gift of such magnitude would offend her. And my husband, being the generous man of God that he is, said, "I'm going to take some time to get the car cleaned up and checked out so that it is ready when God says go."

A few days passed. We prayed and were both so at peace, knowing that although we depended on that car, if God wanted us to give it away, He would somehow take care of us. After all, we could easily get by for the next two weeks with the mom-van as my husband was off work. And after that? Well, we just knew that God would work it out.

> *This generous God who supplies abundant seed for the farmer, which becomes bread for our meals, is even more extravagant toward you. First he supplies every need plus more. Then he multiplies the seed as you sow it, so that the harvest of your generosity will grow. You will be abundantly enriched in every way as you give generously on every occasion, for when we take your gifts to those in need, it causes many to give thanks to God.* (2 Corinthians 9:10-11 TPT)

My daughter and I were at the mall Christmas shopping when I received a call from Tracy. She was calling to arrange our carpool schedule for the next week. She was so grateful for the extra times that I had driven and in no way took that for granted, but she wanted to ask if I could drive again. As I stood in the middle of the department store, she began crying on the other end of the phone. She told me that she had been looking for cars, but she just didn't have a lot of money, and she hadn't been able to find any she could afford. As she continued, my heart began beating faster and harder, and I began shaking. I told her that of course I could drive, and we said good-bye. And I called my husband, still shaking and standing amid happy shoppers. I told him I had our answer, that we needed to move forward with our plan. He said, "Come home and let's figure this out."

The traffic was crazy as we left the mall, with many Christmas shoppers trying to either find parking or hurry home, and I got caught in a traffic flow that took me in an unfamiliar direction. As a result, I ended up driving through a neighborhood I had never even noticed before. As we navigated our way home, suddenly we passed a house with a beautiful black Lexus parked in the driveway with a "For Sale" sign on it. Without a word, I turned around, got out of my van, and took pictures of what I knew to be my husband's dream car. My daughter had no idea what I was doing, and I was still too shaky to tell her.

I arrived home, and my husband said, "Let's go for a walk and talk about this."

Before we walked to the end of the driveway, we both knew what we had to do, and we headed in the direction of Tracy's house. We got there and knocked on the door. Confused, she came out, and my husband said, "Merry Christmas. We want to give you our car. It is a Honda and has a lot of miles on it, but it is in good shape and has a lot of miles left."

Tracy reacted immediately with tears of joy and disbelief, telling us that she had been praying specifically for a Honda she could afford.

The priestly ministry you are providing through your offering not only supplies what is lacking for God's people, it inspires an outpouring of praises and thanksgiving to God himself. For as your extremely generous offering meets the approval of those in Jerusalem, it will cause them to give glory to God – all because of your loyal support and allegiance to the gospel of Christ, as well as your generous-hearted partnership with them toward those in need. (2 Cor 9:12-13 TPT)

A few days later, Tracy's mom invited us over for a holiday meal of lasagna, where she gave us a Christmas ornament that we still hang on our tree every year and a beautiful card. She expressed over and over to us that we were an answer to prayer and that she would, going forward, remember us in her prayers.

> *Because of this extraordinary grace, which God has lavished on you, they will affectionately remember you in their prayers.* (2 Cor 9:14 TPT)

Do you know what we learned in the days to come? You can't outgive God! When He gives you an instruction – no matter how crazy it may sound – He will honor your obedience, and you will ultimately claim the victory! When we determined in our hearts to step out in faith, we had no idea how God was going to provide for us, but we knew He would. Because He always does. After we got home from giving our car away, I remembered the Lexus I had passed on the way home. In the coming days, my husband called the owner and secured a loan from the bank with a monthly payment that fit right into our tight budget. To this day – nine years later – my husband still drives and loves that car. In the meantime, both of our daughters reached driving age – and, as we were praying about how we could provide a car for them, they were EACH gifted a used car from a relative.

> *Praise God for his astonishing gift, which is far too great for words!* (2 Cor 9:15 TPT)

God did shower us with physical blessings through our obedience – but that wasn't the real victory. The real victory was the freedom that we were able to claim from the ways of the world. Sometimes God does ask us to do something that makes no worldly sense, and we respond with many logical reasons why we should say no. When that happens, I encourage you to seek God in prayer and walk in faith, claiming your freedom from the world as a child of God. God has a victory story just waiting for you!

CONQUERING SELFISHNESS

by Julie T. Jenkins

Selfishness is a vision issue caused by our nearsightedness. Today, we wear our "busyness" as a prideful badge, and the busier we are, the less time we allow ourselves to look out to a world in need. We become more and more focused on our own needs and wants and put blinders on, becoming oblivious to what is going on in others' lives.

Selfishness can also be a fear issue. We fear that if we share, we may end up without something we need. The year 2020 will go down in the history books as the year of the COVID-19 pandemic, but let's take a lesson from the absurdity of the toilet paper shortage that, for many of us, marked the beginning of the pandemic. People were in fear, and they were craving control. And someone thought, *what if it comes to the point that I can't get out of my house to buy the staples of life? What will I do without toilet paper?* And the hoarding began. Because of fear and selfishness. Because of the blinders we all put on, allowing us to focus on our own needs and close our eyes to the needs of others.

The apostle Paul teaches us that we can conquer selfishness by imitating the humility of God.

> *Do nothing out of selfish ambition or vain conceit. Rather, in humility value others above yourselves, not looking to your own interests but each of you to the interests of the others.* (Philippians 2:3-4 NIV)

How do we go about learning to value others above ourselves? I would like to suggest two ways: look out and look up!

First, to conquer selfishness, we must look out beyond ourselves and our immediate view. One of the basic tenets of the Christian response is to "serve one another humbly in love." (Galatians 5:13b NIV) We can only serve one another when we intentionally look out to see the desires and needs of others.

Next, to conquer selfishness, we must look up, remembering that God is in control and He is a gracious and generous provider! If we read God's Word daily, He will continually remind us that we do not need to worry – ever! One of my favorite "go-to" verses that I focus on when the spirit of selfishness threatens to creep into my daily attitude is Hebrews 13:5-6. In the NIV translation, it says this:

> *Keep your lives free from the love of money and be content with what you have, because God has said,*
>
> *"Never will I leave you;*
> *never will I forsake you."*
>
> *So we say with confidence,*
>
> *"The Lord is my helper; I will not be afraid.*
> *What can mere mortals do to me?"*

Look out – God has placed each of us in a unique position to be a blessing to others!

Look up – God will never leave you nor forsake you!

KAYLA FOLLIN

is an entrepreneur and creative spirit who aims to serve God through every facet of her life. She is a graduate of Liberty University, where she studied Graphic Design and Photography. She now works as a freelance Graphic Designer and Wedding Photographer.

Kayla has a heart for women's ministry and for using the creative talents that God has given her to provide biblical resources to women across the world. She is the Graphic Designer for Women World Leaders, responsible for the design of *Voice of Truth* Magazine and all published material from World Publishing and Productions Company – including the book you are holding! Kayla also serves on the Women World Leaders' Leadership Team.

Kayla is from Virginia, USA. She loves to travel and enjoy the outdoors. Her favorite place to be, and where she feels closest to God, is in the mountains, especially enjoying a windows-down drive on the Blue Ridge Parkway. She has a passion for film photography and loves to capture the personality of each place she visits through the medium.

BREAKING FREE FROM SEXUAL SHAME

by Kayla Follin

My victory story is one of transformation. I was released from the struggle, addiction, and shame of sexual temptation and sin and given freedom, confidence, and closeness with God. From the age of 14 to 21, shame warped my identity in Christ, which then deeply affected my relationship with Christ. Most of this shame came from an inward place of guilt, but some also came from outside voices in my life. I spent those seven years in a dark inward place. I developed a habit of striving for God's approval, but then falling on my face yet again and sinking deeper into that pit of shame that I thought I had just crawled out of. That is the nature of shame. It doesn't come from God. It comes from the enemy, Satan, who will do anything to lie to us about our standing and identity in Christ. In order to explain my victory story in full, I need to go back to the beginning of it all.

I was a curious child, like most of us were. I grew up with divorced parents and had no real figure of godly relationships or marriages in my life. What I knew about relationships was either from movies that were over-sexualized or from church teachings, which were very harsh and critical. Obviously, these are very conflicting views of relationships, and I remember having that internal battle from the very beginning. I adopted those ideas of fantasy, lust, and desire from movies. Then was taught that sexual intimacy before marriage was the absolute worst thing you could ever do in the eyes of God from leaders at church. Never was I taught the beauty and sanctity of sex in a marriage and WHY it should be reserved for marriage.

You should know that I am a rule follower. I was always labeled as a goody-two-shoes. I held high standards for myself, and most of those were based on my relationship with God. My relationship with Him was the most important thing to me. I desired to know Him and treasured Him deeply. The problem was that I didn't give myself the grace that Christ had bestowed upon me. When I messed up anything, I would beat myself up, thinking God was mad at me. As much as I would say that I knew He still loved me despite my actions, my heart did not fully believe it. I was a perfectionist and strived to do everything in excellence. A heart that knows the grace of God cannot have a perfectionist and striving spirit; those two things do not coexist.

As I grew older, I entered into a serious relationship and was seriously tested with the desire for intimacy. Once again, that striving, rule-follower trait of mine came in strong. Yet, I was not strong enough to avoid the temptation of intimacy. Time after time, I would go farther down the road of intimacy. I would lay in bed at night and cry because I felt so guilty for what I had done. My heart felt empty, and I was afraid God would leave me. The enemy had convinced me that I was not worthy of a relationship with God. I would cry out in prayer, not knowing what to do to stop these desires. Eventually, I would pick myself up, remind myself that I was a saved child of God, and move forward, vowing that I would never commit that sin again. But because my vow was made in my own willpower and not God's strength in me, I would fall yet again. The cycle would start over, and each time it did, that little dark bubble of shame grew in my heart - until one day, it took over.

I had gone as far as I could go down the road of sexual sin. It ate me up inside. I felt like a fraud. I struggled daily, trying to do as much as I could to change the cycle. However, I never dealt with those inward desires that would cause me to sin in the first place. When I wasn't physically sinning with my boyfriend, it would become a battle of mental desires. Eventually, that led to a struggle with pornography. This struggle led to even more shame because, in my mind, that was even dirtier! I felt alone and unable to talk to anyone because I had never heard of a girl struggling with viewing pornography. The subject was always directed at boys during youth camp sermons, so I logically assumed I was the only female tempted in this area. My feelings of unworthiness and filthiness took over my identity. I felt tainted. I was sure that I would never come out of the dark pit that I was stuck in.

I finally mustered up the courage to tell someone about my struggle. I told them everything I had done with my boyfriend and how stuck I felt. I was hoping for answers, just waiting for someone to tell me how to undo the mess that I felt so tangled in. Unfortunately, my confidante heaped more judgment, conviction, and shame on me, not understanding the weight of shame I had already put on myself. I became even more sure that those things were true now that someone else had spoken them over me. Not only did I think those things about myself, but now I had confirmation that someone else thought those things, leading me to believe that God thought those things about me, too. I shoved down any sense of grace I felt from God, and now I chose to feel only His judgment. The striving cycle continued, and I felt like I would never find freedom from these lustful desires that ruled my heart.

After several years of struggle, I had finally had enough. I had been reading books, devotionals, and blogs about these issues for years. But it wasn't until I realized the difference between guilt and shame that things started to change. You see, guilt is a healthy emotion that comes from God. When we are saved children of God, we have the Holy Spirit dwelling within us. The Holy Spirit serves as our compass in some ways. He convicts us when we disobey God's Word and encourages us to follow His heart and His will for us.

Shame, however, is not from God. Shame comes when Satan turns healthy guilt into an identity-shifting sense of unworthiness. Shame tells us we will never be enough. It tells us that there is no way out. It tells us that we are tainted, ruined, and will never be the same. Shame never brings a healthy, God-driven way of repentance but rather digs us deeper into the hole of our sin. In contrast, guilt leads us to repentance. And we should be thankful for that conviction! Conviction is one of God's methods to gently discipline us for our own good and invite us back into His presence.

It took years for that truth to set in. I earnestly continued to seek the Lord and learn more about His heart. When I went to college, I started to realize that what I believed about God's heart was not true at all. Yes, He is a God of justice and wrath. But this is what I was missing: As a saved child of God, Jesus took that wrath for me on the cross. I had known this all along! But my heart chose to believe the lies of the enemy instead of the truth of the Gospel. My perspective took a shift. The next time I fell back into that trap of sexual sin, I did not try to get back up in my own power. I had tried that for too long and knew that it would get me nowhere. Slowly, the amount of time I spent beating myself up for my mistakes lessened. My study of God's Word began to ring through my ears. My idea of who I was in God's eyes was being rebuilt and renewed, and with it, my identity in Him.

I have broken this healing process down into a few steps, which I am reluctant to do because sometimes that can encourage a striving spirit. I know it did for me at times. But, these points are what propelled me into freedom in Christ.

First, I had to redefine my understanding of the character of God and how I viewed my standing with Him.

Malachi 4:1-3 (CSB) states,

> *"For look, the day is coming, burning like a furnace, when all the arrogant and everyone who commits wickedness will become stubble. The coming day will consume them," says the Lord of Armies, "not leaving them root or branches. But for you who fear my name, the sun of righteousness will rise with healing in its wings, and you will go out and playfully jump like calves from the stall. You will trample the wicked, for they will be ashes under the soles of your feet on the day I am preparing," says the Lord of Armies.*

The Lord confirms here that He will judge those who are arrogant and commit wickedness against His commands. BUT, those who fear the Lord will be HEALED by the "sun of righteousness" (that's Jesus!). I do not need to cast judgment on myself when the Word of God says that I will be healed and set apart from His judgment because my heart fears Him.

Two other passages that deeply changed my perspective on the character of God were Nehemiah 9 and the book of Hosea. Both passages tell of the relationship between God and Israel. Despite the many times they disobey the Lord purposely, He always welcomes them back into His loving arms. Nehemiah 9:17 (CSB) states,

> *They refused to listen*
> *and did not remember your wonders*
> *you performed among them.*
> *They became stiff-necked and appointed a leader*
> *to return to their slavery in Egypt.*

But you are a forgiving God,
gracious and compassionate,
slow to anger and abounding in faithful love,
and you did not abandon them.

Did you read that?! He is slow to anger and ABOUNDING in faithful love, never to abandon them. Now that lie that Satan was telling me over and over again about God giving up on me because I had failed too many times is debunked! Despite their stubbornness to obey His commands, He still forgave and cast His love on them. I encourage you to read the rest of this chapter in Nehemiah. It is a beautiful picture of the people choosing things contrary to God's will, reaping the consequences, and then they coming running back to God as He is waiting there with open arms. We also glean from this chapter that when we cry out to God, He hears us and that He is gracious and compassionate to His children.

The character of God is also there to rebuild and restore us. Not only does He welcome us into His loving arms, but He promises not to leave us there! He promises to walk with us in the dark places, heal us, and set us out to dance in His joy. Jeremiah 31:3-4 (CSB) states:

the Lord appeared to him from far away.
I have loved you with an everlasting love;
therefore, I have continued to extend faithful love to you.
Again I will build you so that you will be rebuilt,
Virgin Israel.
You will take up your tambourines again
and go out in joyful dancing.

Not only does He rebuild us, but He strengthens and restores us. 1 Peter 5:10 (CSB),

> *The God of all grace, who called you to his eternal glory in Christ, will himself restore, establish, strengthen, and support you after you have suffered a little while.*

How beautiful is that! The God of Grace restores, strengthens, and supports us in our weakness. I'm so grateful for God's Word and how it has reshaped my view of the character of God. He is not out to make us feel like we are nothing more than dirt on the ground. We are chosen children of God, called to His eternal glory, and loved deeply by our Heavenly Father. These are the truths that set me free from my dark pit of shame. He has restored my heart, mind, and soul from the addictions and traps that I was stuck in for so long. He promises that to you too, friend.

The next step I took toward healing was to continue praying that my desires would align with God's desires for me.

This is the ultimate struggle as sinners! Our fleshly desires constantly pull us away from the safety and security of God's will. It is so important to ask Him daily to realign our hearts and minds to match what He has for us in each season of life. Our deep love for Him should propel us to honor Him and the commands He gives us in His Word. 1 Thessalonians 2:11-12 (CSB) states,

> *As you know, like a father with his own children, we encouraged, comforted, and implored each one of you to walk worthy of God, who calls you into his own kingdom and glory.*

We are called to walk worthy of God in FREEDOM. Not in a striving spirit, but in one that loves God more than our desires. He knows we won't be perfect – that's why He sent His Son for us. He encourages and comforts us in our daily fight to honor Him.

Finally, allow someone to walk through your struggles with you and support you in your healing process.

Whatever you may be struggling with, I encourage you to find someone trustworthy who has a strong relationship with Christ to whom you can tell your struggles. It is so important to pray that God would bring the right person into your life for this purpose. Keeping it balled up inside will only breed more shame. Ephesians 5:8 (CSB) brought so much encouragement to my heart when I was working up the courage to talk to someone. It states,

For you were once darkness, but now you are light in the Lord. Walk as children of light— for the fruit of the light consists of all goodness, righteousness, and truth— testing what is pleasing to the Lord. Don't participate in the fruitless works of darkness, but instead expose them. For it is shameful even to mention what is done by them in secret. Everything exposed by the light is made visible, for what makes everything visible is light. Therefore it is said:

Get up, sleeper, and rise up from the dead, and Christ will shine on you.

We are called to expose the darkness in us to the light of Christ! When everything is exposed and made visible by the light of Christ, there is space for

His grace and healing. Invite someone into this journey with you to support, encourage, and speak truths over you.

My prayer is that these steps – understanding the character of God, aligning your desires with His, and allowing someone to walk through your struggles with you – will lead you on the path to releasing your troubles to the Lord.

My journey to victory and freedom in Christ was filled with many trials. But I am so thankful for those trials because they taught me more about God's character and how deeply He cares for me. God has rebuilt my purity and identity in Him. He has given me the freedom to forgive that person who spoke shame upon me. He has given me the freedom to forgive myself for the shame I inflicted upon my own spirit. His Word has taught me about godly relationships, marriage, and sex. It has taught me how to fight those fleshly desires and keep my heart focused on His. I hope this encourages you in some way. We all experience some type of shame. Yours may not look exactly like mine, but I hope these passages and truths will remind you of how valued you are by your Heavenly Father and that there is nothing you can do to change His mind about you!

If you are not a believer in Christ, I want you to know that God cares about you. He sees your pain and struggle. He has not forgotten about you. When we are in such depths of shame, we often feel like we are not worthy of love or redemption. The truth is we aren't worthy of redemption! Romans 5:8 (CSB) says, "But God proves his own love for us in that while we were still sinners, Christ died for us." The beauty of the Gospel is that even though we are sinners, unworthy of eternal life, God sent His Son to die for us on the cross. He felt the wrath of God for our transgressions. But, death did not defeat Him. He rose from the dead and is seated with God in heaven. This gift is available for us, and it is free to receive at any moment. When you surrender your life to Christ, you find freedom from sin and death. He is waiting for you, friend.

Conquering Bad Choices

by Kimberly Ann Hobbs

How many of us have made a bad choice in our past, which, at the time we thought might have been the right thing to do? I certainly have. Sometimes these choices have consequences that have to be dealt with or ramifications that can affect us later in life. Bad choices or wrong choices can drastically alter our path if we are not careful. How can one rectify a bad choice? Personally, I found victory regarding even my bad choices when I allowed God to open my eyes to see things more clearly. My perspective on what I thought were mistakes or terrible times in my life were turned into helpful memories that shaped me into the person I am today. God uses everything for good for those of us called with a purpose by Him. And we all have a purpose. Have I looked back and wished I had never made mistakes? Yes, but I did, and I thank God for His grace and mercy, which turns everything into good, constructive understanding.

When I changed my perspective on following my own choices and realized I needed to switch direction, I turned to God, asking Him for His infinite wisdom to begin making the right choices. God can put any of our puzzle pieces together if we pray for His wisdom, and that's exactly what we all need to do.

And if anyone longs to be wise, let him ask God for wisdom and He will give it! He won't see your lack of wisdom as an opportunity to scold you over your failures, but He will overwhelm your failures with His generous grace. (James 1:5 TPT)

Can God fix our bad choices? I believe He can and will fix yours as you grow in Him and trust Him with your whole heart. Remember, if you wish to conquer wrong choices, do not put your trust in people, places, or things, or even in yourself. Put your trust in God.

> *Trust God with all your heart and lean not on your own understanding; in all your ways submit to Him and He will make your paths straight.* (Proverbs 3:5-6 NIV)

Immerse yourself in the wisdom of God's Word, and you will soon be victorious over wrong choices, find yourself, and manifest fruit as you make the right choices in your life.

. . . .

LILLIAN CUCUZZA

resides in Land O' Lakes, Florida. She has been married 39 years to organist Dave Cucuzza, whom she met when she bought her first organ and lessons from him.

As a highly respected and accomplished Regional Vice President for a financial services company, she enjoys coaching people to financial independence.

Lillian's passion is nature photography and serving God. Her photography accomplishments include First Place at the Florida State Fair in 2020 and 2021, the first two years she competed! She was recently awarded First Place by the Florida Press Association in the Division A Reader-Generated Photo category of Weekly Newspapers for her iconic photo of the Neowise Comet over the Grand Tetons. Lillian's work is regularly published in The Laker/Lutz News, and her photo-art is showcased in an art gallery in Dade City, Florida.

Lillian is the featured photographer and author for HIS Creations, LLC, a Christian photo-art and crafts online store. You can view her photos and nature books at www.HisCreationsLLC.com.

As a contributor to Women World Leaders' magazine, *Voice of Truth*, she uses her photography and writing talents to glorify and honor God for His beautiful creation.

Physical Healing Through A Personal Meeting With God

by Lillian Cucuzza

"What was I thinking?" I asked myself as I slapped my forehead. It was only a week before my second trip to Israel in three years, and I just remembered there would be one exceptionally long day on our feet in Jerusalem. In the excitement of preparing for this trip in June of 2010, I completely forgot about that arduous ordeal of standing and walking an entire day on my first trip in 2006-2007.

You might be thinking, "what's the big deal?" It is not a big deal unless you have Plantar Fasciitis and heel spurs in both feet, which I had been suffering with for over four years. My condition caused extreme pain first thing in the morning. My husband helped me out of bed every morning and was my support until my foot tendons stretched enough so that I could stand on my own. Then, as the day progressed, if I was on my feet for any length of time, they started to fatigue and hurt so badly that all I could think about was getting off my feet. That cycle repeated itself every day for close to five years!

I had been to a podiatrist for treatment, which consisted of expensive orthotics and a cortisone injection in each heel ten days before my first trip to Israel in late December 2006. Those shots put me on crutches for two days, and I still went on that trip with great trepidation, worrying whether my feet would hold me up. Fortunately, I was so excited about being in Israel and walking where Jesus walked that I was not focused on my feet, even though there was still pain and fatigue throughout that first trip.

However, those cortisone injections do not last forever. Now, as I reminisced about that first adventure, I realized that I had no time for any new injections to prepare for this second trip. All I could do was pray that I could survive the excruciating pain, especially on the longest day in Jerusalem.

I must tell you a little bit about our first trip so you can appreciate the second. We visited all the sites where Jesus walked. We listened to our extremely knowledgeable guide teach and preach everywhere we went. The tour was packed with educational information and Bible lessons.

It was a 10-day winter trip, from December 27, 2006, to January 4, 2007, and it snowed the night before we got to the Holy City. It was thirty degrees Fahrenheit, just below freezing, the next morning as we began our long walk and day in Jerusalem. We started on the Mount of Olives, where our guide preached for an hour and a half. Because everything was wet from the snow that melted, there was nowhere to sit while he preached, so we stood the entire time. That was just the beginning of the day. It was the longest and toughest day of the trip for me. I finally knew what my mother meant when she said, "My dogs are barking!"

When we got back home, our pastor suggested a dinner party to review what we enjoyed the most. As we went around the room sharing our experiences, the last person to speak revealed that she had gone to Israel with a specific purpose: to have a personal meeting with God. I felt a bit embarrassed that I had gone with no thoughts in mind of what I wanted to do or see - I was just excited to go to the Holy Land and walk where Jesus walked.

She shared that when our guide suggested we find a private spot in the Garden of Gethsemane to spend some time in prayer, she knew exactly what she would pray and ask God about. But before she got to her private place to pray, God answered her prayer directly! She had her meeting with God before she could even ask! God already knew what was on her heart and addressed it. I do not know what that prayer request was, but I was in awe of the fact that she had a personal meeting with God in Israel! All I could think of was how cool it would be to have a one-on-one meeting with God in His Holy Land! I know you do not have to go to Israel to have a private, personal meeting with God, but I also knew that if I were given a second chance to go back, I would be more purposeful and thoughtful of personal time spent with the Lord.

The second trip to Israel, quite different than the first, was in June 2010. Our Israeli tour guides were deeply knowledgeable and experienced. We took our time at each site in prayer and worship. We had a busload of people from our church, with the youngest being a teenage boy and the oldest close to ninety years old.

While we were at the Mount of Beatitudes, our pastor suggested we each find a private place to spend some time by ourselves in prayer and God's Word. Afterwards was a luncheon in Ein Gev of Saint Peter, which consisted of fish (Tilapia) from the Sea of Galilee. I sat next to the teenager. He confided with me that he had a touch from the Holy Spirit at the Mount of Beatitudes. He said when he closed his eyes to pray, he saw Jesus in his eyelids. He also felt a "heat ball" roll up his arm while praying, even though he was sitting under a tree in the cool shade. He thought maybe a bee had stung him, but when he looked around, he did not see anything.

I was curious, so I asked would he mind sharing exactly what he prayed about. He prayed he would know for certain that he was saved. I felt like a knife had just been plunged into my heart and twisted. I was devastated and in tears for the rest of the day. I knew that this young man just had a personal meeting with Jesus, and I was so happy for him. But I was also a bit jealous. Was my personal meeting with the Lord to be through the eyes of this teenager? Would I have to settle for his experience? Now I was beginning to question my salvation. I could not focus on anything else for the remainder of the day.

We arrived in Jerusalem two days later and would tour the entire city on foot the next day. I knew I was in for a grueling day on my feet.

By 10:30 am, we were in the heart of the city, having walked from the Mount of Olives, down the Palm Sunday Path, into the Garden of Gethsemane, through the Kidron Valley and into the Lion's Gate, also known as Stephen's Gate - where Stephen was stoned. We then went into the Church of St. Anne, well-known for its amazing acoustics, where we sang hymns and heard the beautiful singing reverberate for seconds. After, we came out of the church and took a break on some benches outside. I was so thankful for those benches because my feet were killing me. I could go no further, and it was only 10:30 am.

Next to those benches outside the Church of St. Anne was the site of the pool of Bethesda, which means *house of mercy*. This ancient pool was no longer a pool above the surface but is now about 60 feet below ground level. In Biblical days, it was known for the healings that happened there.

> *By the Sheep Gate in Jerusalem there is a pool, called Bethesda in Hebrew, which has five colonnades. Within these lay a large number of the sick—blind, lame, and paralyzed [waiting for the moving of the water, because an angel would go down into the pool and stir up the water. Then the first one who got in after the water was stirred up recovered from whatever ailment he had].* (John 5:2-4, HCSB)

Our pastors used that break as a prayer time for all those with physical ailments. Many in our group had serious diseases, and some were terminally ill. As the pastors prayed, they asked us to raise our hands if we had a physical need. As much pain as I was in, I just could not bring myself to raise my hand. I looked around and saw my friends there who were dying of breast cancer, heart disease, brain tumors, melanoma, leukemia, and other deadly illnesses. I felt guilty because I only had a pain of inconvenience. They were dying and holding on for dear life with every ounce of courage and strength they had. How could I possibly be so selfish to raise my hand and think of myself at a time when these people needed real healing? As I prayed, asking God to touch and heal each of them, I was in so much pain I meekly raised my hand. I saw and felt the pastor touch my hand just as he did with everyone who had their hand up during that powerful time of prayer.

When the pastors finished praying, they explained that we might have felt tingling, heat or cold, or another unusual sensation. However, we were not to be alarmed but instead be excited to have a touch from Holy Spirit. I did not feel anything, but I was hopeful that those who were seriously ill did, and I looked forward to hearing the stories of healings later. Meanwhile, I was thankful for the chance to give my aching feet a break.

As we stood up to move on to the next stop, I was totally refreshed and energized. I had no pain whatsoever! I felt like I could run up the hill! I looked around to see if anyone else experienced the same thing. I took a few steps – no pain. I immediately knew something happened during that prayer time. (I later realized that the lack of pain WAS the feeling or sensation from Holy Spirit I experienced.)

As we walked uphill toward Antonia Fortress, I could no longer hold back my excitement. I elbowed one of the pastors, saying, "I think something happened back there!" He did not know that I was in so much pain from Plantar Fasciitis and heel spurs. He was happy for me, but I tried to temper my excitement and told him, "We'll see how long it lasts before my feet start hurting again. The real test will be in the morning when I get out of bed." He just laughed.

About fifty feet later, I told another pastor, "Hey, I think something happened back there! I feel like I have so much energy I could run up this hill!" I told him my story, and he got excited. Again, I did not want to get too excited, only to be disappointed later, so I told him, "We shall see if it lasts when I get home. Maybe it is only good while I am here in Israel." He smiled, probably thinking I was just like doubting Thomas. My energy level lasted all day, and I did not have any more pain that day as we walked and toured the rest of Jerusalem. I was happy to survive the longest day.

The next morning, without thinking, I jumped out of bed on my own. I did not even think to wait for my husband to help me out of bed. It was just a natural action to jump out of bed. When I landed on my feet, I realized that I had no pain for the first time in five years! That is when I finally understood - I had been healed! At that moment, I realized I had my own personal meeting with God the day before! I could barely contain myself! I have been praising Him ever since!

> *One man was there who had been sick for 38 years. When Jesus saw him lying there and knew he had already been there a long time, He said to him, "Do you want to get well?"* (John 5:5-6, HCSB)

That is exactly what Jesus was asking me at the pool of Bethesda. Do you want to get well? I did not hear those actual words, but Holy Spirit prompted me to raise my hand if I wanted to get well. I felt guilty and selfish, thinking I was taking the healing away from others if I raised my hand. Instead, I was not trusting and allowing God to be God! I was putting God in a box with my limited thinking of how much I thought He could handle. I had to swallow my foolish pride and accept God for who He is. I had to accept that He loves us all, even me, and wants to shower us with His indescribable, unfailing love, mercy, and grace. He can handle anything and everything at the same time! After all, HE IS GOD!

In Mark 9:22-23, NIV, a man begs Jesus to heal his son.

> *"...But if you can do anything, take pity on us and help us." "If you can?" said Jesus. "Everything is possible for one who believes."*

Wow! There was absolutely no chance of claiming victory in Jesus without raising my hand, totally trusting and believing in Him!

I did not have to get into the pool to get well. Neither did the lame man in John 5:7-9, HCSB.

> *"Sir," the sick man answered, "I don't have a man to put me into the pool when the water is stirred up, but while I'm coming, someone goes down ahead of me." "Get up," Jesus told him, "Pick up your mat and walk!" Instantly the man got well, picked up his mat, and started to walk.*

Like the lame man, I just had to accept the invite. I humbly raised my hand to submit and trust in God with all my heart, was healed, and started to walk again without pain! This picture holds true for our salvation, too. We can do nothing to save ourselves, earn our way into Heaven, or heal ourselves from our sin. It is simply by believing, submitting, and trusting in God's saving grace, by faith alone, that we are healed and saved. Only Jesus, God Almighty Himself, could do that for us! Oh, what a Savior!

My story does not end here. It was only the beginning of my healing. In late 2017, I again started having severe heel pain and Plantar Fasciitis in my left foot. It shook my faith. I could not understand how God's healing could be temporary. I believed that if He healed me, it was permanent. I began to wonder if I had really been healed in Israel at all or if it was just a fluke. I started doubting that I had experienced a true healing by God. Then I began to worry what all my friends would think if I had this foot problem again. Would this shake their faith? Would this move them away from accepting Jesus as Lord and Savior? Would they think I was just a nutcase? Would they believe that God was real? What would they say? Who could I even talk to about it? All sorts of questions, fears, and worries wreaked havoc in my mind and spirit. I was under attack from the enemy.

I saw a podiatrist who did x-rays and confirmed the diagnosis. He tried to push my foot back towards my ankle, and it would not bend at all. When he said I had a severe pronation or supination, I said, "Speak English, please." He explained that is the term used when your foot takes an extreme roll inward or outward, which happens with a stumble or fall. I jumped for joy on his examining table and exclaimed, "Praise God!" and explained.

Six months earlier, I had a terrible fall in Indianapolis during a company convention. As I walked down the sidewalk, I did not see that the half-shaded sidewalk had separated into two levels, and my left foot rolled off severely towards the outside of the foot. I fell headfirst toward the sidewalk. It took six months for the effects of that fall to develop into a new case of Plantar Fasciitis. I was thrilled with the explanation the doctor gave me because I now had full confirmation that my Jesus did not let me down. He physically healed me in Israel, and this new condition happened because of that accidental fall!

What a relief!

The doctor explained that the injury caused the calf muscle to tighten, which caused the plantar tendon to tighten and create heel spurs. So, I only needed to stretch the calf muscle and tendon every morning by pulling my foot towards my ankle and holding for about thirty seconds before getting out of bed. Eventually, it would loosen the muscle and tendon, and the pain would go away!

Within two months of stretching exercises, I was no longer in pain. But to set the record straight, I did not know about nor do any of those stretches the first time I had Plantar Fasciitis and heel spurs. I now know for certain that God truly healed me of my affliction! It was nothing I did but everything God did! Praise God for His everlasting love and unfailing kindness!

I learned from this experience that the stories in the Bible are not just stories. They are real-life lessons that are as relevant to us today as they were back then. The Bible is a living, breathing document meant to help us understand and overcome our condition today. It is the Word of God, a love letter directly from Him, and allows us to claim victory and freedom in Christ Jesus! It is a personal meeting with God every time we pick it up and read it!

CONQUERING LIES

by Kimberly Ann Hobbs

Daily, our minds are barraged with many thoughts. But do our thoughts align with God and what He says in His Word? We need to be guarded because some of the thoughts in our minds can be lies that the enemy wants us to believe.

We can be victorious over a struggling thought life. Science says we have approximately 50 to 70 thousand thoughts that swim through our minds each day. That is a lot of thinking. Yet God tells us to take EVERY thought captive. We need to pay attention to what we are thinking about and determine if our thoughts agree with what God tells us in His Word or if they are lies from the pit of hell.

The enemy can speak lies to you in whispers that will take you from the victorious path God has intended for your life. Don't listen when the enemy tells you:

- You're not important.
- You're worthless.
- You're a victim.
- No one likes you.
- You're all alone, no one cares.
- You're a failure.
- Your words have no value.

We need to protect our thought life like we protect our valuable property. We must stand guard against the lies the enemy wants us to believe. Let's look at a command from God's Word:

> *We demolish arguments and every pretension that sets itself up against the knowledge of God, and we take every thought to make it obedient to Christ.* (2 Cor. 10:5 NIV)

We must know God's Word to fight back against the lies of the enemy. Throughout God's Word, He equips us with ammunition to fight back against the lies. If the enemy tells you, "You are weak – you can never accomplish the task before you," you must fight back with truth that says, "NO! According to Isaiah 40:31, in Him, I am strong."

Learn God's Word and use it as a weapon to fight and conquer the lies you are bombarded with daily.

> *Then you will know the truth and the truth will set you free.* (John 8:32 NIV)

. . . .

TINA KADOLPH

lives her life advocating, empowering, educating, and providing safety for survivors of human trafficking.

Tina has overcome many of life's greatest tragedies. With God, she has taken the pain from those tragedies and turned them into purpose. She's now a co-owner of Palate Coffee Brewery and Palate Bubs & Ice Cream. She is the president and founder of Love Missions Global, a ministry that advocates for victims of human trafficking. Tina's oversight includes a safehouse in South America for children brought out of sex slavery and a local life center for teaching life skills to survivors in Florida. Her story has been featured on CNN and other news agencies.

Tina's goal in life is to use her pain to protect, educate, and prevent human trafficking, so others never have to go through what she has.

Tina resides in beautiful Florida with her amazing husband of 37 years. She has two beautiful daughters and six grandchildren. She loves traveling, serving God, doing mission work, and just hanging out with her family. She is thankful for every day God gives her to show his love to others.

LOVE IS...

by Tina Kadolph

I never thought love was possible for me.

I never believed in love. I thought it was a fairy tale, like Cinderella. I longed for Prince Charming to ride up on a white horse and carry me away to a safe castle, where no one could reach me. I'd be safe, far, far away from all those who wanted to harm me, just like Cinderella. The prince saved her from her wicked stepmom, and they lived happily ever after. But as much as I longed for it, I knew it would never happen. Love wasn't real. I truly believed that.

You see, my life didn't start out like a lot of other little girls who had moms and dads who loved them. I didn't have a mom or dad who would do any-thing to keep me safe, whether it meant risking their own lives or not. I didn't even have a mom or dad who showed me love.

I was sold and thrown into the world of sex trafficking at four years old. Yes, you read that right. I wish this were not part of my story, but it is.

As a child, I always dreamed of having what I thought looked like a normal life. I dreamed of being Marsha Brady from *The Brady Bunch*; I really loved her long, blonde hair. I had wavy, frizzy, brown hair - and that was not cool at the time. Or maybe I could have a mom like June Cleaver on *Leave It to Beaver*, who always kept a clean house and had delicious-looking food on the table every morning, noon, and night for her family to eat.

My house looked nothing like that. Most of the time, we had to rummage to find what we could feed ourselves. A lot of the time, I had to help my younger brothers. It sure didn't look like a pretty table with a smiling mom and yummy, nutritious food.

I did not have much of a childhood. Many of my childhood memories have been blocked out due to the trauma, but what I do remember was abuse, physical and emotional, starting at my earliest memory of four. I do not remember why the transaction happened or how much my mom got for me when I was only four years old; I just remember the horror of what happened when that man stepped into my room. Those details are embedded into my mind like it happened yesterday. I remember what the house looked like, the wallpaper on the wall, and how the furniture was laid out. So much detail is embedded into my mind. I find this odd because other parts of my childhood and the abuse I endured are completely blocked out. Thank goodness God designed our minds to protect us. I was later diagnosed with Post Traumatic Stress Disorder (PTSD), a natural diagnosis, the doctors said, caused by the trauma that I had experienced.

Living in that environment, I associated love with abuse. Some of the men who came into my room told me how pretty I was and that they loved me. Then they would hit me, burn me, and rape me. Love was so distorted. How was I to know what love looked like? It certainly looked nothing like what I wanted, even though I longed for it. It does not make sense to want something you don't understand and haven't experienced. I now believe that's because God puts that desire for love and relationship in us. He wants us to love Him and have a relationship with Him. Those first experiences of love usually start with your parents. It is one of the many reasons that nurturing and love are so important from the start of life. Deep down, I longed for a mom, a dad, and a safe place to live without the worry of what was next.

At the age of 15 or 16, I ran away from home, thinking I could do life better on my own without my mom controlling the abuse that happened to me. What was I thinking? Sadly, so many young people living in dysfunctional families think the same thing I did, and there is a trafficker just waiting for them. The trafficker knows they have probably been abused, are looking for family love and acceptance, and have basic needs that need to be met - like a roof over their heads and food. The trafficker also knows that they are worth the investment of time. They groom these victims by showing them love and affection and giving them gifts until they have them eating out of their hands and will do whatever the trafficker wants. The child has this false sense of what love really is and begins to think the trafficker loves them, that finally, their dream has come true - they are being loved. Until the other shoe drops. And guess what? The abuse begins. Same abuse, only different person. This time not your mom, but your boyfriend and his friends. He reminds you that you have nowhere to go. He tells you no one will ever want you or take care of you like he is. And you believe it. When he hits you, he tells you he is sorry, and you believe it. You cry until you can't cry anymore, and he beats you and says he is sorry and that he loves you, and again you believe it. Pretty soon, you do whatever he says because you hope you will make him happy so he doesn't hurt you anymore, and just like with your mom, if you do not, there will be horrible consequences.

Then one day, you decide to say "no more," you're done. You're leaving. He hits you over and over again and then puts a gun to your head and says he is going to kill you. You will only go through that door in a body bag. If only it could be true and this life can be over. He hits you, screams at you, and calls you all kinds of nasty things.

Little do you know, your neighbor hears what is happening and calls the police. And they take him to jail.

Seriously, what is love?

He is gone for now. Will he be back, and is he going to kill me? How long will he be gone?

He had been gone for a week, and I was feeling more and more hopeless. Living in such fear of what was to come.

What was next for me? Where do I go from here? I was so tired of the abuse. That's all I had known for 18 years and all I could think about over and over in my mind.

So, I decided. I would end my life. I had all the drugs I needed; it would not be hard. Just take them and go to sleep forever.

> *The thief comes only to steal and kill and destroy. I came that they may have life and have it abundantly.* (John 10:10 ESV)

At that time, I didn't know God was at work; everything was about to change. As I planned my suicide. I did not know then, but God was getting ready to intervene, and my life would be forever changed.

As I looked at the drugs in front of me, a friend called. Well, not really a friend, but we were both at some of the same parties and involved in the same lifestyle. She asked me if I wanted to go to a party with her. I figured, why not? I didn't have anything to lose at this point. Today that seems so stupid and reckless. But to a traumatized 19-year-old, it made perfect sense.

I did not have a license; I had never been allowed to drive. But I hopped in my ex's van since he wasn't able to use it and recklessly drove myself to the party. Everyone was having a good time drinking and doing drugs. There were lines of coke on the tables, cans of beer everywhere, and I wasn't interested. I just felt so sad and miserable. I even had a Bartles & Jaymes berry wine cooler in my hand, my favorite. That should have covered up my feelings, it always helped before, but nothing was working. I just kept thinking about going home and ending this crappy life.

As I was in this very deep train of thought, a guy walked across the room and smiled at me. I'd seen him around at other parties, but we never interacted. I thought, *Really? Just turn your little self right back around, and don't bother me.* This was not anything I wanted. I did not need another guy in my life to continue what I was just running from. I didn't need another guy to act nice to me, only to hurt me again.

He said, "Are you alright? You look like you need help."

I said, "I'm not alright, but I certainly don't need your help."

So, he said, "That is fine, but if you change your mind, give me a call." And he handed me a slip of paper, which I shoved in my pocket without looking at.

When I got home - I have no idea how I made it home - I sat back at the table and looked at all the pills still waiting for me. Tears rolled down my face as I reflected over my childhood into my teen years to this very moment. I had a few good memories from my childhood, but in most of them, my mom was drunk and was doing things we thought were funny. Looking back now, it's sad because those memories that I thought were fond were not really - because she was drunk and still putting us at risk. But I still thought it was fun, and it was, compared to what could have been happening. There wasn't much hope for me to hold onto and make me want to live this incredibly sad life I had lived.

As I picked up a hand full of pills, I felt an urge or nudge to call that guy. I had forgotten about him until that moment. I looked in my pocket, and there it was on that little piece of paper, HIS number.

I yelled out loud, "No, I do not want to call him. EVER." But the urging just got stronger. Today, I believe that was God. I looked at the paper and dialed the number. Carl answered the phone. I could hear him say hello. I didn't answer right away, but finally I said hi. I said, "It's Tina; you gave me your number at the party."

He was shocked because of how I had treated him when he gave me his number.

I said, "You're right, I do need help."

He said, "Do you want to have coffee?" Which is funny, because now we own a coffee shop.

I said sure, and we made a date to have coffee the next day. So, I didn't take the pills. I still thought I would, but for now it could wait.

We met for coffee at a little cafe and talked for hours. He was kind and listened so well. I didn't tell him everything about my past, but I did tell him I was coming out of an abusive relationship. He just listened with a kindness I had never known. The next day he had a red rose sent to me with a note that said, "Never let anyone determine your worth. You have so much value and beauty you do not see in yourself. You are truly priceless."

I cried because no one in my life had ever said words like this to me or made me feel I had any kind of worth. I always felt hopeless and that I had no value. I believed I was nothing but trash from trash.

But suddenly, deep inside, hope started to stir. It was a feeling I had never known before. God is so amazing. Both of us had healing to do. Especially me. But with God, we know all things are possible, and, as crazy as it may seem, I believe God knew what He was doing when He put us together.

At the beginning, I tried so hard to push Carl away. I got in his face and screamed at him to hit me. I pushed as hard as I could because I believed he would, it was just a matter of time, and the other shoe would fall. It is the way it always happened in the past. This time I was wrong. He never hit me and always showed me love and kindness and patience. It took me about three years, but I finally believed he was who he was. Either that or he was just plain crazy!

We lived together before we got married because I didn't want to be tied to him or trapped to him. Still waiting for that shoe. After three years we decided to get married. I didn't get a beautiful wedding; we just went to the courthouse in Oklahoma City where Carl was doing a job at the time. With my 30-dollar mall kiosk wedding ring and ivory, thrift store dress, and his pawnshop wedding band, we asked a stranger to be our witness and headed to the courthouse to get married. Once we were married, we then went to Chili's restaurant and had a drink to celebrate. I thought love would look so different. My wedding would be so different. Honestly, I never thought I'd be married. Who would marry me?

But I can't explain how excited I was to actually be married to this wonderful guy. I really might have a chance at life.

Loving a woman with so much baggage, trauma, and trust issues wasn't an easy task. But Carl never gave up on me or us. He continues to be my biggest fan today. Encouraging me that I can do anything I put my mind to. He says, "You can't have survived what you have and not be the strongest woman I know." That one is still hard for me to swallow, but I do believe God saved me for a reason. I also know that I can persevere through life's toughest challenges. I know that by using my past, God has developed a strength in me that not many have.

We really wanted kids one day, but we weren't sure that was a possibility. I had a lot of damage from what I had endured as a child, and when I was 18, I was told by a doctor that I would never be able to have kids. But God is in control, and now Carl and I have two beautiful daughters. What a beautiful gift God gave us.

Love is so much different than what I longed for. So much better than the Bradys or the Cleavers from those television sitcoms I grew up watching.

Love is... a God who gave His one and only Son so that I could be made clean and all the ugly could be wiped away.

> *For God so loved the world, that he gave his only son, that whoever believes in him should not perish but have eternal life.* (John 3:16 ESV)

Love is... a God who loved this abused girl beyond what she could have even imagined, this broken girl, turned into a broken woman.

Love is... a God who brought a loving, kind man into my life and who has stood by my side for 37 years.

Love is...a God who restores and redeems broken hearts, and heals damaged lives.

And after you have suffered a little while, the God of all grace, who has called you to his eternal glory in Christ, will himself restore, confirm, and strengthen, and establish you. (1 Peter 5:10 ESV)

Love is...Victories and freedom only Christ can give.

I'm thankful that Jesus has shown me what real love looks like. It started with a man named Carl, who led me to a God named Jesus. I can share my many victories because of the healing Jesus has done in my life. There is nothing or no one too broken for Him.

But thanks be to God, who gives us the victory through our Lord Jesus Christ. (1 Corinthians 15:57 ESV)

CONQUERING BITTERNESS

by Julie T. Jenkins

I have an ongoing struggle with sugar! With varying degrees of success, I am constantly trying to cut sugar from my diet. Recently, this quest led me to ask Google, "What stops sugar cravings?" One of the answers was bitters.

Bitterness steers us away from sweetness.

While that is useful information for avoiding sugar intake in my diet, it's also a warning for our attitudes. Allowing bitterness to infiltrate our spirit can keep us from being kind and loving and lead us away from living a life of joy and peace as God intends.

Emotional bitterness can begin when we are hurt and develop further as we allow our anger to smolder, even causing long-term issues such as anxiety, depression, and an obsession with retribution. It's easy to see how the growth of bitterness can infect our attitude and change our demeanor. Additionally, bitterness can quickly spread from one individual to another.

The writer of Hebrews warns us in Hebrews 12:14-15,

> *Make every effort to live in peace with everyone and to be holy; without holiness no one will see the Lord. See to it that no one falls short of the grace of God and that no bitter root grows up to cause trouble and defile many.* (NIV)

So how do we keep that bitter root from growing?

Paul gives us the warning to "get rid of all bitterness" in his letter to the Ephesians, and he gives us a simple formula to do so:

> *Be kind and compassionate to one another, forgiving each other, just as in Christ God forgave you.* (Ephesians 4:31-32 NIV)

Simple. But not easy.

To be kind and compassionate, we have to put our own entitlement aside. When we are justifiably hurt, it can be natural for that hurt to smolder into bitterness. But if we choose to react in kindness and shower the one who hurt us with compassion, we can douse the embers of hurt before they erupt into flames of bitterness.

To be forgiving means releasing our ill feelings for the one who hurt us. This may seem downright impossible. And as humans, operating in our own capacity and strength, it IS impossible. However, we CAN forgive by accessing the power given to us through Jesus Christ. Jesus suffered the most unimaginable and unwarranted pain as He died for our sins; yet in dying for us, He offered us both His forgiveness and the ability to forgive others.

Conquering bitterness requires us to not allow hurt to fester within us, which requires kindness, compassion, and forgiveness attained through the power of Jesus Christ.

If you feel a bitter root growing in your soul, do not give it the opportunity to infect you or those around you. Instead, pray to God, asking Him to release you from the burden of pain that has been inflicted on you. You may need to go to Him again and again – sometimes those pesky weeds have quite deep roots! Don't give up!

Just as bitters in our diet steer us from ingesting excess sweets, so too will sweetness in our spirit steer us from bitterness. If we intentionally, by God's power, incorporate kindness, compassion, and forgiveness in our lives, we can conquer the root of bitterness!

. . . .

STEPHANIE J. FINCHER

has served as a ministry leader and contributing writer for *Voice of Truth* magazine, a publication of Women World Leaders. During the years of prioritizing family and raising children, Stephanie assisted with informal writing opportunities which sparked a desire to develop the skill, though publishing her work was not an immediate goal. She used writing as a tool to encourage others, while assisting some small organizations in writing policies and procedures to maximize operations. She holds a degree in education and was active in a hybrid-style homeschool structure until all four of her children were grown. In later years, Stephanie owned a business with her husband and was heavily involved in the marketing and management side of operations. She has served on several ministry boards over the years and is honored to write a piece of her adoption story in preparation for a future book.

Stephanie has been married to her sweetheart for 35 years, enjoys running, tennis, and family adventures when her clingy, but adorable shih-tzu lets her out of his sight.

UNPLANNED VICTORIES – AN ADOPTION STORY

by Stephanie J. Fincher

Dedicated to my mother Julie*, one of the strongest women I know. You led this journey from first loving me on your knees.

Victory...a concept rather obvious to most, yet individually defined depending on the lens through which it is viewed. It can and usually does change over time and with experiences that life brings. The rise of its anticipation builds upon fresh energy and an ideal vision created in our mind's eye. Attempting to list every possible victory for every person would be never-ending, though a few common pursuits are shared among many. Such ambitions might include the strategic and goal-driven climb to career success, an inspired dream that propels talent to fame's glory, the joyous hope of holy matrimony, or even a long-awaited child pursued in the heart of prayer - which happens to be where my own story begins.

Life has many defining moments that may be unrecognized until long after they've come and gone. We look back and understand something significant, sometimes with the weight of sorrow and sometimes in awe. Sometimes both! Though God foreknew the detailed design of my entire life (as He surely knew yours), He shaped my beginning through the earnest prayer of a strong, lively lady named Julie, my dear mother and forever friend. And in

God-like fashion, He took her prayer and connected it to the selfless action of a woman I would later know – Sarah*, my birth mother. Two different lives walking very separate paths were intersected in a plan arranged by the heart of God. Unexpected heartache for one and fulfilled celebration for the other collided in an unconventional sisterhood of sorts. How is it that God would create a triumph of beauty in both of their worlds and mine? Come with me into the story, authored by One who works without limitations and who invites you to see Him in your own story. If victory's hope has been lost or abandoned in the weeds of heartache, there is a God who is able to sprout something new and uncover fresh manifestations of things yet to come.

> *Eye has not seen, nor ear heard, Nor have entered into the heart of man The things which God has prepared for those who love Him.* (I Corinthians 2:9 NKJV)

> *Jesus replied, "What is impossible with man is possible with God."* (Luke 18:27 NIV)

. . . .

Troubled Transitions – Sarah

Young Sarah grew up in a challenging family environment—certainly not a refuge for the jolt of an unplanned pregnancy. It made sense, then, that she would end up staying in the home of a nurturing couple who ministered and cared for unwed mothers. It was a safe place of encouragement that would support her when the time came to release her baby in the ultimate gesture of selflessness. To a bystander with no concept of such a pivotal and emotionally charged decision, it would be easy to hastily judge with frowning disapproval - "How could someone *give away* their baby, their own flesh and blood?" At that time in society, children born out of wedlock were outside the norm of acceptance and certainly evoked a not-so-hushed gossip of social opinion. Surely this intensified the very delicate moment that releasing such a gift would bring. But deeper than that was a fallout that required more than just a "determined will to conquer." How would emerging faith find the courage to step above heartache's grip and survive the crushing squeeze? It would be through the purposed, higher intervention of a gracious, loving Lord. Though Sarah was unaware throughout her journey, a tender presence and loving care of God watched over her life and the one she carried. The stage had been set for a powerful victory that only God Himself could perfectly arrange.

> *The Lord will watch over your coming and going both now and forevermore.* (Psalm 121:8 NIV)

> *See, I am doing a new thing! Now it springs up; do you not perceive it? I am making a way in the wilderness and streams in the wasteland.* (Isaiah 43:19 NIV)

. . . .

Anticipated Promises – Julie

For Julie and her husband Rick*, adoption was not part of the original family plan, but God was introducing a new direction for them. As an act of faith, they boldly stepped forward and agreed that adoption could be a wonderful way to begin a family. The months of preparation became busy for the couple as they filled out forms and application papers and dreamed of being parents. The normal stressors of life were further heightened as they anticipated the agency's final home visit – the last box to check to be approved as a "fit family" for a newborn. Of course, Julie wanted all to look perfect, be perfect, and sound perfect, and her tenacious attention to each detail would ensure that it was. The months spent praying on her knees at the empty rocking chair fueled her desire for a "just-right" atmosphere for the agency visit. She had already sensed that the Lord had affirmed His will to answer her prayers at the right time, and she figured it wouldn't hurt to add a few "made-to-order" details along the way...

"Please, Lord, a baby *girl*...dark brown eyes...a touch of baby-soft hair... healthy...sweet-natured..."

> *I wait for the Lord, my soul waits, And in His word I do hope.* (Psalm 130:5 NKJV)

. . . .

Many people like Julie and Rick choose to adopt, and sometimes, a couple already has children when adoption is pursued. The Lord may stir a husband and wife's heart, moving them to further grow their family through this remarkable process. It is a beautiful promise of unconditional love and acceptance, securely tied with irrevocable rights as a child of the family. It illustrates the magnificent position we receive upon accepting Christ's gift of salvation that is complete with every right and access as sons and daughters of the Most High God.

> *God decided in advance to adopt us into His own family by bringing us to Himself through Jesus Christ. This is what He wanted to do, and it gave Him great pleasure.* (Ephesians 1:5 NLT)

For the Son of Man [Jesus] came to seek and to save the lost. (Luke 19:10 NIV)

Now if we are children, then we are heirs—heirs of God and co-heirs with Christ, if indeed we share in his sufferings in order that we may also share in his glory. (Romans 8:17 NIV)

. . . .

Rising Conflicts – Sarah

The heat of the warm summer day faded into a calm evening sky as labor pains progressed quickly for Sarah. It was just after midnight when a healthy baby girl increased the population by one more in the small southern town. The hospital staff were swift to usher the new mother out of the delivery room, away from the sight and sounds of the crying newborn. Sarah was not supposed to see the baby since this was an adoption case, but everything happened so quickly that she caught a glimpse of the dark-haired bundle. Nurses dutifully wheeled Sarah into another small room that bore no evidence of the new life that had entered the world just moments before. There were no celebratory laughs amid tears of joy, no proud papas posing for photographs, no beaming grandmas doting gleefully over mama and baby. The air sat numbingly still as Sarah's mind and body summoned rest and sleep, and it was a welcome break to drift away in silent slumber.

The following morning, a beautiful Sunday, the sun beamed brightly through a small window as Sarah picked up the phone and dialed quickly. She wanted to let the baby's father know that she had given birth to a daughter.

"How are you doing? Is the baby all right?" he inquired. She assured him that she and the baby were well, as far she knew since she had not really seen the baby. Sarah talked for a few more minutes and sighed deeply as she hung up the phone. Her thoughts began to replay the prior night's hours leading up to the birth. The baby girl who had been kept out of sight was nearby, and Sarah knew exactly where to find her. Reaching for her robe, the young mother made her way down the hallway that led to the busy nursery. Peering through the fingerprint-smudged glass, Sarah smiled lovingly at the tiny patients lying sweetly in clear bassinets, though her little one was crying persistently as occupied nurses attended to others. It annoyed her that nursery staff were not responding to *her* baby's cries, and she tapped the glass for attention and pointed toward the infant. She fixed her gaze resolutely on the little one's face and quietly cherished the next few moments. She could not shake the rising need to hold the baby, which tugged strongly on her motherly instincts. She would soon be signing papers that would permanently separate her from the life she had carried, and she longed to cradle the one she would forever call her "special little angel." Yes, she would definitely ask for the infant upon returning to her room. She had six whole weeks to change her mind about the adoption, and she intended to savor this private moment, her *only* moment as a mother holding her daughter.

I will be glad and rejoice in Your unfailing love, for You have seen my troubles, and You care about the anguish of my soul. (Psalm 31:7 NLT)

The Lord is near to the brokenhearted and saves the crushed in spirit. (Psalm 34:18 ESV)

Sudden Surprises – Julie

Some adoptive families wait years for their dream to become a reality, so when the heart-stopping call came with the news that a baby was ready just months after the application approval, Julie was beside herself. The adoption agency said that she could see the baby the very next day, and Julie had an arsenal of excited, nervous questions for the lady on the phone.

"Was the baby a boy or a girl?!"

"You have a girl!" came the reply.

"How old is she?!" Julie pressed anxiously.

"She is six weeks old, plus a couple of days."

"Does she have any hair?!" exclaimed Julie.

The woman on the phone laughed, "Goodness gracious, we have to save *some* surprises — you can find out tomorrow when you see her! Oh, and one more thing – once you see the baby, you'll have to wait another 24 hours before taking her home - it's standard policy for all adoptions."

Julie barely slept a wink that night, and she and Rick were at the agency's door before it opened the following morning. Julie was about to burst as they were ushered into a room where the baby girl was waiting in a crib. The social worker gave few details about the birth parents and focused on identifying birthmarks on the infant along with other important information adoptive parents needed to know. It was an overwhelming and extraordinary morning for the couple. They could hardly take enough pictures as the baby was passed back and forth between their arms. The answered prayer was more than Julie could soak in as the small office room overflowed with laughter and rejoicing over the surreal moment!

> *Give thanks to the Lord of lords, for His loving-kindness lasts forever. Give thanks to Him Who alone does great works, for His loving-kindness lasts forever.* (Psalm 136:3-4 NLV)

. . . .

Critical Doubts – Sarah

Time is credited as a healer of wounds, but has time ever carried a child that it gifted to a stranger? Sarah's heart and emotions were in knots over the days and weeks after leaving the hospital. "I can't do this," she lamented to the kind couple who had housed her over the past months. They had become family to her and were in the process of helping her step back into a "normal" rhythm of life. "I know I've signed those papers, but I want her back – I want to keep my baby! I can work and raise her myself." Her mind knew that she had done the right thing, but her heart rebelled in solid protest.

The compassionate couple understood and expected this internal conflict and urged Sarah to stick with her decision. It was for the best, they explained, and Sarah did not have the means to provide for the ongoing demands to care for and raise a child. It was not what Sarah wanted to hear, but she undeniably knew the couple was right, and she also knew that the toxic part of the family environment she had left would be unchanged if she returned. She did not want to raise a baby in such conditions, but it didn't lessen the terrible sense of grief and loss. At the same time, it was comforting to know that her child would be in a family that very much wanted and loved her. Lingering within, however, were thoughts that would be ever-present as time marched on. *Would her "special little angel" ever know who Sarah was...would she even want to know? If told of her adoption, would the girl feel abandoned, rejected, and resentful of Sarah's decision?* These questions and others would shadow Sarah through the years among more challenges to come. But as young Sarah found hope in Jesus and grew in her faith, she would pray for and think about the little girl year after year. And year after year, God steadily prepared hearts to experience the depths of His care and unmatched love and mercy!

> *"For the revelation awaits an appointed time; it speaks of the end and will not prove false. Though it linger, wait for it; it will certainly come and will not delay."* (Habakkuk 2:3 NIV)

> *And may you have the power to understand, as all God's people should, how wide, how long, how high, and how deep His love is. May you experience the love of Christ, though it is too great to understand fully. Then you will be made complete with all the fullness of life and power that comes from God.* (Ephesians 3:18-19 NLT)

. . . .

Redemptive Power

Time, as always, did march on and brought revelations of twists and turns that only Hollywood filmmakers might dream up! I grew up quite differently from what might be a natural conclusion to this story. My mother, Julie, was put in a terrible position that jeopardized my adoption when I was sixteen months old. It was out of her control, but never out of God's, which He demonstrated by making a pathway where there wasn't one! In addition, the years revealed startling truths of my beginnings that brought distress into lives who were unaware they were connected to me. One person in particular perhaps suffered the most pain, though I'll never know to what depth. This compassionate soul has extended overwhelming love and tenderness toward me when it would have been easier to walk away. I can hardly grasp it. It is its own victory – a miracle, really – that testifies to God's manifest power in a heart that surrendered to receive that power.

The truth is that God did not cause the disturbances sprinkled across my storyline. But He did lovingly intervene and connect new relationships in unlikely circumstances. I marvel at what He has done! I have come to know dear people on each side of my biological family, and I am grateful for the privilege of knowing them as the gift they are to me. I have had the honor to see how God shaped little victories in preparation for the sweetest purposes on the other side of brokenness. In a greater and higher way not fully understood, He has woven a supernatural ending worthy of heavenly applause. And He longs to reorder *your* circumstances for the greatest story, too, because His love for you is personal, immeasurable, and unchangeable!

> *For I know the plans I have for you," declares the Lord, "plans to prosper you and not to harm you, plans to give you hope and a future.* (Jeremiah 29:11 NIV)

. . . .

Victory's Call to You

My story and other trials in life have shown me that turbulent waters inevitably find us and can threaten our solid footing. We may be unexpectedly swept up into a rising panic, signaling a search for a quick escape route. It is here where critical decisions are made that influence our lives as well as others' lives. It is also here where victory and hope call out, and His name is Jesus. Simplistic sounding? Perhaps so, but ever-powerful when stormy waters wash over hope and ravage peace. If invited into your life, the Prince of Peace will not only sustain your spirit but will lift your willing heart to higher ground. Emotion, doubt, and seeds of fear may still attempt an ambush deep within, but the new foundation has stability because God is there. The unrelenting hold can be released to Providential hands that fight for you and help you. Trusting in God's strength and not our own, we find calm under His constant vision and promised presence. And as His child, it is *irrevocable.* Just as earthly parents are not always visible, yet we know they are "there," the Lord *really is with us,* ready to repurpose the broken and unveil a hidden victory.

There is *life* to experience beyond your circumstances, and value in what you walk through. Find freedom and healing in how it can be used and determine not to "sit down at the door of God's purpose and enter a slow death through self-pity."[1] Your victories, both large and small, are waiting to be discovered. And someone else needs to hear about yours in order to find theirs!

> *Now thanks be to God who always leads us in triumph in Christ, and through us diffuses the fragrance of His knowledge in every place.* (2 Corinthians 2:14 NKJV)

[1] Taken from *My Utmost for His Highest**by Oswald Chambers, edited by James Reimann,© 1992 by Oswald Chambers Publications Assn., Ltd., and used by permission of Our Daily Bread Publishing, Grand Rapids MI 49501. All rights reserved.

*Author's Note: Names in the story have been changed to protect the privacy of individuals. Any similarities or details related to another person's circumstances are coincidental.

CONQUERING JEALOUSY

by Kimberly Ann Hobbs

Having a spirit of jealousy is like a downward spiral leading to death. Jealousy kills our attitude and our relationships, and it kills our true inner joy and peace. Jealousy also leads to discontentment, bitterness, anxiety, and even depression.

All the ugly feelings that arise by not conquering this behavior could present a travesty of being unable to love others the way God intended us to. The enemy has a way of crushing our spirits so we can't reach others. Being jealous is a sin that leads to a life of pain and makes us unable to work for God.

The Bible speaks against jealousy. The enemy wants us to chase after everything except God. Chasing what others have, copying how others behave, or coveting another's friends could all be symptoms of a jealous spirit. Your value does not come by comparing yourself to who someone else is or to what they have. Your value and security come from God alone. When the ugliness of jealousy comes, remember you are made for better things. The Bible says:

> *Wrath is cruel, and anger is outrageous; but who is able to stand before envy?* (Proverbs 27:4 KJV)

Envy is destructive. God is clear in His Word that jealousy is a quick route to destruction and pain in our lives. By breaking free from the feelings that arise from a jealous or envious spirit, you will be free and rewarded with the joy you are truly seeking. Jealousy does not belong in the heart of a

Christ-follower. God created each of us unique, our lives are different from other's lives, and we are all loved and special in God's eyes. We need to understand and accept that we are fearfully and wonderfully made by an extraordinary God.

If we live defeated by jealousy, we can't help others. In order to have freedom from jealousy, we need to move the attention off ourselves and put the focus on others. Please do not compare yourself to others nor desire what they have. This adds to the ugly feelings that you will have over them. Jealousy holds you in captivity. Pray and ask God to illuminate issues of your own heart, and pay attention to the godly answers He shines on your pathway so you can respond quickly, following the light He provides. God made you to be you and not someone else. He gave you things that others don't have. Be content in your heart with what you've been given.

> *A heart at peace gives life to the body: but envy rots the bones.* (Proverbs 14:30 NIV)

Victory over jealousy is yours when you truly can say and believe Psalm 139:14...

> *I praise You because I am fearfully and wonderfully made; Your works are wonderful; I know that full well.* (Psalm 139:14 NIV)

Please remember to demonstrate gratitude in your life daily and avoid the dangers and sinful behavior that a jealous spirit brings.

. . . .

CAROL ANN WHIPKEY

is a published author in three books. She is a Christ follower, and much of her time is devoted to serving in the Women World Leaders ministry as a writer and encourager through her uplifting, joyful spirit, wise guidance, and love for writing.

Carol enjoyed her career as a beauty consultant and working in an accounting position at UPS, and is now retired.

She is also an artist, trained by the world-renowned woodcarver, Joe Leanord, whose work is in the New York Museum of Art and at Disney in Paris and the USA. As a hobby, Carol spends much of her time carving horses, birds, and other commissioned work that comes her way.

Carol lives in her own park-like setting on 52 acres in Thompson, Ohio, with her husband, Mel. She is the mother of four, including her first-born child, Kimberly Hobbs of WWL. She is also a grandmother of six and a great grandmother of seven.

It Is for the Children

by Carol Ann Whipkey

> *But when the Father sends the Spirit of holiness, the one like me who sets you free, He will teach you all things in my name. And He will inspire you to remember every word that I've told you.* (John 14:26, TPT)

God reminds us by the Holy Spirit of the things He wants us to remember, and so for that reason, I am writing this story - to show how God held me in His hand, seeing me through this life since I was born.

While lying awake and praying one night, thinking about things in my past, God put into my spirit the ability to recall an incident in my life, which I believe He wants me to share. The freedom I have in Christ now allows me to recall a traumatizing incident from my past. My story brings up thoughts of how we should take precautions for our children's safety.

I am certain God whispered to me to share this story so that others may understand how we can carry the trauma of horrifying childhood experiences into adulthood. But God. He brings victory where victory is needed. I can still remember this incident clearly, but God has comforted my thoughts through His merciful manifestation in my life over the years. He delivered me to overcome this painful incident in my childhood.

I was no more than five years old. There was a man, a very tall man. He may have been so tall because I was so little looking up at him. He seemed to be nice. I remember my dad and mom laughing and talking with him inside our home. It was a sunny day, and the man asked me if I would like to go for ice cream. Of course, I said yes, and I remember begging - like any child to their mother - to please let me go. My mom said yes, and I recall skipping out to his car and getting inside.

I sat on the front seat, but I could not see anything out the window; I was just too small. I remember the older model car that I was sitting in had exceedingly small windows. The man told me to stand up on the seat so I could look out the window to see, so I did. Standing in the front seat of his car, we drove off!

Joe was the name of the man. He wore a white shirt with suspenders and an old-fashioned hat like they wore back in those days; it was in the 1940s. I can remember I was wearing a brown and green pleated skirt with suspenders so my skirt would not fall. It may have been on a Sunday because I was all dressed up and not wearing my usual play clothes. Joe and I drove out of the driveway, which was exceptionally long due to living out in the country on acreage. I turned on the seat to wave to my mommy out the window, with a big smile on my face, as the car drove away from our home.

I do not remember Joe saying anything to me on our way to get ice cream. The drive was incredibly quiet, and I politely waited for what seemed to be forever to get to that ice cream stand. After a while of driving, we pulled into a big area with nothing around except trees. Even as a child, I knew something was wrong, this was not an ice cream store, and my heart began beating extremely hard, and I started to cry. The man said, "If you stop crying, I will take you for ice cream." He told me we had to walk down this path to see something first. We walked down a very skinny pathway with bushes on both sides and excessively big trees. Everywhere I looked, there were trees. Afraid, I began to cry again. The man picked me up, and we walked deeper into the woods while he kept talking about how big the trees were and how pretty the sun was shining through them. I was crying hard by then, and I could sense that he was getting nervously agitated with me.

The man continued carrying me in his arms while I kept saying, "I want my mommy; I want to go home."

The man named Joe said to me, "Ok, if you stop crying, I will take you home." I tried to stop, but I could not.

He stopped at a tree while holding me in his arms. It was an exceptionally large white-barked tree. He told me that it was something called a paper tree. He started peeling the tree to distract me telling me the peelings were what paper was made from. He called it a parchment tree; I think. I do not think I cared anything about this peculiar tree that Joe was trying to amuse me with, and I continued crying while he gripped me in his arms. All I wanted and re-membered at that point was wanting to be back in my home and see the face of my beautiful mommy.

As I am writing this, my insides are starting to tense up, and my stomach is turning upside down. I know today how extremely wrong the situation was and that Joe was a bad man. I knew it then, and I can feel it now again. He put me down and grabbed my hand harshly. He was pulling me because I was resisting and crying louder. Oh, how I wanted to go home! I remember all the leaves that covered the ground. I remember the sticks and twigs and baby trees and green things that were everywhere around me. We were not on the path anymore; he was taking me deeper into the woods. I cannot remember at this point if I fell or if he made me sit on the ground, but all I know is I was in the dirt, terrified as I kept crying harder for him to take me home.

Out of nowhere, there came a voice that yelled, "Hey, what are you doing?" Drenched with tears on my face, I looked up. Out of nowhere, I saw a big brown horse and a policeman riding it. The policeman towered above me and asked me why I was crying. The man immediately spoke up and said it was because I fell. No, I thought to myself, it is because I want to go home!

Instantly I saw the beautiful horse. I became mesmerized by it. The beautiful shiny coat that sparkled like jewels all over the animal diverted my attention. To this day, I can remember that horse and the policeman that rode on it. I could even see his kind but alarmed face in my eyes. The policeman said I could pet his horse while he would talk to the man. I did not pay much attention to their conversation at this point, but I remember the man took something out of his pocket and gave it to the policeman. Then I remember the policeman telling me that this man would take me home and I would be alright. He walked us all the way back to Joe's car. Then the policeman put me inside the car, and while I sat inside, the policeman talked to Joe. I have my own ideas of what was being said between Joe and the policeman that day. The policeman went around to the back of the car and stayed there for a minute, near the license plate. Now, as an adult, I believe he was getting the information on the vehicle and from the man.

As this man and I were in the car together again alone, he began to tell me I could not tell my mommy about what happened because she would get mad at me and not love me anymore. He said she would never believe me. He continued to tell me this over and over. He said that all he wanted to do was show me the trees; he did not know why I was so bad; this was all my fault. He told me that my mom would be mad at me for being a bad girl and causing problems so that the policeman had to stop us, and that is why he did not want to take me for ice cream! He told me not to tell my mom about the horse because she would really get mad. After all, I could have gotten hurt from petting him. Joe had me so ridden with guilt and fear that I would not dare tell my mom! As we pulled into the long driveway home, I was just so happy to be home and be safe that I hid what happened deep down inside me and never brought it up again...

Until...

A few years later, my brother and I were ready to make our first communion. In the Catholic Church, we had to go for training, called catechism classes, before we could take our communion. The classes lasted two weeks. When they were complete, we were able to get dressed up like the bride of Jesus and have communion. One beautiful Sunday, I was able to wear the pure white dress my mom had bought me while my brother wore his white suit. We had been taught at the classes that if we confess our sins to God, we would be as white as snow, inside and out. I wondered to myself, *Was my sin of being a bad girl with this man something to tell God I was sorry for?*

Before we went to the altar we sang a song. I still remember it because it meant so much to me. It goes like this, "Oh Lord, I am not worthy that Thou should come to me, but heed the words of comfort, thy Spirit yield shall be, and slowly I'll receive the bridegroom of my soul, no more by sin to grieve Thee but by Thy sweet control." I still sing this song sometimes, and I can recall it like it was yesterday. I remember receiving Jesus into my heart, believing that I was saved but not understanding what it really meant to be saved until later years. I am trying to remember if I confessed what happened to me as sin back then, but I cannot remember. The man had me convinced that I was such a bad girl and bad girls do not go to heaven. It scared me, but I can clearly remember the horse and the angel riding it. And God proved to me years later it was an angel sent by Him to save my life that day!

Thinking back on my questions of sin that arose as I prepared for my first communion, God was showing me how He keeps us in His will and brings us peace as we focus on Him. At every age of life, God holds us in His hands.

Back to my story, but many years later, I am about 15 now. I was standing at the kitchen sink doing dishes in our old farmhouse in Ohio. We had a picture window right in front of our sink; on the windowsill sat a card. The electric bill used to be sent out on cards, like postcards. The card was meant to be split in half, one side for the company and the other side for the homeowner, who would rip the card and send the appropriate half with the payment. Reading the card, I saw the name Joe Z. Something inside of me started trembling again, and I ran to the bathroom and got sick. I knew in my heart it was that man!

After calming myself down, or the good Lord calming me at that moment, I went back, got the card, and in my trembling hands took it over to my mother, asking who this man was. My mom responded, "That's your dad's good friend, but he moved away to California and asked us to pay the bill for him." She proceeded to tell me he was my godfather. I could not believe what she was saying. I could not bring myself to say anything else to her, but the past fear welled up inside of me again! The voices in my head continued, "It's your fault, you are the bad one," and resounded over and over. Joe's voice was haunting.

Moving forward in my story again, I am now married with a daughter who is four years old. One day there was a man walking down the street in our neighborhood. My daughter was in the front yard playing with the neighbor boy. This man appeared, dressed all in white. He wore a white suit, had white hair, a white hat, and even carried a white cane! He had a white book in his hand, and he stopped to talk to the children right in front of our house. As quickly as he came, he turned away. And then he completely disappeared in a matter of seconds. I yelled outside in a panic, "Kimmy, come in the house!"

Asking my daughter what the man said, she responded, "Mommy, he talked about church and a book," but she could not remember exactly what he said.

Immediately memories flooded my mind of my own incident, because my sweet innocent little girl was confronted by a man she did not know, and it scared me for her. I shuddered to even think that what happened to me could happen to her or anyone else. Desperately compelled out of fear of what could have happened again, I called my mother. My mom had always given me good advice. "Non," that's what we called her, "I have something to tell you that I've held on to for years." Still thinking she would blame me somehow, I had to tell her what I had been hiding deep inside of me for so long and how fear arose through seeing my baby girl in harm's way. I unfolded the whole story. We both were crying hard when she shared that she could not understand why I never told her about this horrific occurrence. I had to explain to her how Joe, the man, made me so scared, instilling so much guilt that I could never tell anyone, especially her! We both had an exceptionally long cry. As she told me back then, you never have to be afraid to tell your mother anything, and if you do not tell your mother, tell God. God already knows everything about you and will help you in any circumstance! I never forgot that great advice coming from my mother. I felt the heavy burden lifted that day, and a freedom I have never felt in all my years of growing settled on me. I have told few people the story but felt led to share for the little ones that no longer have a voice to tell their story!

God spared me and protected me with the policeman and horse that bright sunny day. I decided to tell this story because there is evil in this world, always wanting to destroy the plan that God has for us. If the evil one can make us feel guilty or take away the blame for the evil things done, he wins.

Our Lord and Savior is the only way we can truly be saved from the deceit and lies Satan says about us. There will always be predators in this world to push people to do bad things and who will work to destroy the plans that God has for us in our lifetime.

For we are God's handiwork, created in Christ Jesus to do good works, which God prepared in advance for us to do. (Ephesians 2:10, NIV)

I plead with you to take hold of your children and grandchildren and encourage them to tell you things you do not even want to know. There was victory for me when I finally shared my story with my mom, and she gave me godly advice. Tell God everything. He already knows everything about you. This brought me freedom. As we can all tell God our Father anything, I encourage you to teach your children that they can tell you anything as well. Please keep the communication lines open with your children and grandchildren always. Show them how much you love them and tell them you will never be mad at them for telling you anything. I cannot explain how horrible it was to have kept this inside me for so many years.

If sharing my story can help one person think or spare one child's life, I have achieved my goal by writing about my haunting past. I also want you to know in your heart your loving Father in heaven has known you from the beginning, as He says in the scripture.

For He chose us in Him before the creation of the world to be holy and blameless in His sight. In love He produced into us to be adopted as His sons through Jesus Christ, in accordance with His pleasure and will. (Ephesians 1:4, NIV)

Even before He made the world, God loved us and chose us in Christ to be holy and without fault in His eyes! If you know the Lord, never let anyone tell you that you are "the bad person," especially when someone pushes their evil onto you. You are God's creation; He knew you before you were born. His plans for you are written in His word.

> *Many, oh Lord my God, are the wonders You have done. The things You plan for us no one can recount to You; where I to speak and tell of them, they would be too many to declare.* (Psalm 40:5, NIV)

> *"For I know the plans I have for you,"* declares the Lord, *"plans to prosper you and not to harm you, plans to give you hope and a future."* (Jeremiah 29:11, NIV)

Jesus tells us in Matthew 19:14, Luke 18:16, and in Mark 10:14, let the children come to Me. Do not stop them! The Kingdom of heaven belongs to those who are like these children!

Take care of your children, believe them when they tell you things; most children will not make up terrible things. Most of all, always tell them and assure them they can tell you anything, even if it is bad. Make sure they know you will love them always! My mother did this for my brothers and me, and I do this for my children and grandchildren! I correct them if they are wrong, but I love them through all situations! I have told you a part of my heart, and I pray you understand what this message is trying to convey. It is for THE CHILDREN!

CONQUERING WORRY

by Julie T. Jenkins

Worry happens when we allow our minds to dwell on something that has gone wrong or could go wrong. There is a LOT that we could worry about every single day – in our personal lives, the lives of those we love, even regarding issues that continue to develop worldwide. The problem with worry is two-fold: it brings us down, and it hinders us from being productive.

Most obviously, worry leads us away from a spirit of peace and joy, bringing us down. Worry doesn't just come upon us when things look threatening – the devil is a bit trickier than that. I tend to be gripped with worry when I leave for vacation. Even when I know that I know that I know I have checked everything off my list and prepared for every imaginable circumstance, the "what if's" still enter my mind, threatening to rob me of the joy of my upcoming adventures.

Our preoccupation with worry saps our joy and can also prevent us from contributing to a given situation in a way that God intends. You see, sometimes God doesn't just present the solution to a problem, like a magician, but instead, He works through His children, empowering us to be the solution. When we allow ourselves to dwell on what could go wrong, we don't spend as much energy on actively seeking to make it right. The devil wants to incapacitate us, tying our hands as our minds fret. But God wants to empower us with courage and strength that we might work with Him to claim victory.

So how do we move away from the worry that threatens to steal our joy and stop us from doing all that God has called us to do? Paul tells us in Philippians that we are to rejoice, let our gentleness be evident, and not be anxious. (Phil 4:4-5) Then he gives us a formula to accomplish this.

- **Pray and give thanks!** (Phil 4:6) Go to God with a grateful heart for all He has already done.

- **Allow God to fill you with His peace!** (Phil 4:7) Trust that the One who sees the unseeable and who knows the unknowable will be with you in every circumstance and is in control.

- **Focus on the good!** (Phil 4:8) Fill your mind with thoughts of who God is and what He alone can do. Our God is our Provider (Jehovah Jireh), our Peace (Jehovah Shalom), our Healer (Jehovah Rapha), The Most High (El Elyon), Strong (Elohim), and Almighty (El Shadai)!

- **Put into action all that you have learned!** (Phil 4:9) Give God control of every step as you take action, walking in obedience and using every tool He has provided you.

Following these steps will empower you to reclaim your mind, establishing peace and productivity as God intended, and conquer worry. Take that, Satan!

. . . .

KELLY WILLIAMS HALE

is a writer, speaker, and leader. She is passionate about equipping believers to be brave. Kelly is a graphic designer by profession, but her heart's desire is to encourage women. As a clarity coach, Kelly empowers Christian women to overcome self-doubt, worry, and fear so they can live a life of significance, courage, and confidence.

Kelly's journey has been one of highs and lows, and through it all, she gives all glory to Jesus. God has blessed her with this one life. She's living it as her gift back to him.

Kelly loves sushi, Almond Joy candy bars, and guacamole. She is the happiest when she has Christian music playing; anything by the band *For King & Country* is her favorite.

Kelly is happily married to Buddy and has a unique understanding of parenting, raising three only children – Christie, Dallas, and Austin – all born about a decade apart! She's also a Mimi of three and lives in Jacksonville, Florida, where they enjoy the beach and their Husky, Phoenix.

FORGIVEN

by Kelly Williams Hale

> *They triumphed over him by the blood of the Lamb and by the word of their testimony.* (Revelation 12:11 NIV)

I was smack dab in the middle of writing, sharing my story of God's grace and how He blessed my obedience, when I heard this verse. I was feeling pretty good about my message. Well, up until this moment anyway.

Have you ever heard God's voice so clearly? I have, and today was one of those times. You see, while I was writing about how God blesses obedience, I was reminded of a time when I was very specifically disobedient.

While wearing my earbuds and happily traveling back to house-sitting for my uncle, God told me that now is the time to share a part of my testimony that only a handful of people know. He reminded me that, "My grace is always more than enough for you, and my power finds its full expression through your weakness." (2 Corinthians 12:9 TPT) My story exposes my weakness, but I pray it will also encourage you, sweet Sister. His grace is sufficient.

When we feel like we have messed up so badly, sinned beyond redemption, Jesus is there to remind us that He paid the price for our sin. He overcame the world and my *past, present,* and *future* mistakes – by His blood.

When Jesus was crucified, His blood covered not only my sins, but your sins, too. If you're reading this, I believe He has a message for you. There is nothing so bad that we have done that cannot be redeemed by the blood of the Lamb. It has taken me 27 years to share this, but I was reminded that to defeat the enemy of our soul, the one who would like nothing more than for all of God's children to live in shame and silence, we must share our testimony.

I was raised in a family of six, the oldest of four kids – the only girl. My youngest brother is only four years younger than me, so you can imagine the challenge my mom had getting us all to church, much less getting us to *pay attention* once we got there! It was a struggle for three boys to sit still – together – for an hour, but it was my job to help. I realize now I was a bit bossy, but I believe God was developing my leadership skills, even then!

I knew the Lord. I knew what was right and wrong, and I followed the rules. Looking back now, I see my faith was based more on religion than a relationship. In my mind, I had to be a good girl for God to love me. I was baptized at 11, but honestly, only because my other church friends were being baptized – and I wanted nothing more than to be accepted.

There wasn't much talk about Jesus – that I can remember. But I know that He's been with me since the very beginning. (John 1:1) I often hear people say they feel like God has left them, but I know now we are the ones who drift away, especially when we haven't developed the relationship that God so desperately wants with us.

Do you ever feel like God is waiting for you to mess up? Do you imagine He's a father-like figure eager to dole out punishment for not following the rules? A God who keeps a checklist of sins; one more strike, and you're out? If you do, let me tell you, the enemy is such a liar. (John 10:10)

While I may not have imagined our Heavenly Father to be quite so strict, I felt like I needed to *do* all the right things. And when I did sin, there was so much shame and guilt – it was easy to imagine that my behavior and choices earned me a seat in the back of the class. How could God love me when I was such a screw-up?

Sweet Sister, before I continue, please know that God loves you so much! If you're a mother, can you imagine sending your son to die for your grumpy neighbor or the co-worker who gets on your last nerve or the homeless man on the street corner? God loved *us* so much that he literally sent his *only* son to die for us. Jesus suffered and was ridiculed and made fun of. He was crucified and rejected. For you. And for me.

God *is* love. That's been one of my more recent revelations. Isn't it funny that we can think we know something, but then, like lightning, we are struck with a new understanding? Then it becomes real and personal. "So, what does all this mean? If God has determined to stand with us, tell me, who then could ever stand against us?" (Romans 8:31 TPT)

God's love *is enough.* (1 John 4:16) That means we can depend on Him. We can trust Him. And even when we sin, we are forgiven because Jesus paid the price. (Romans 5:8) And while we can accept God's forgiveness, forgiving ourselves is often harder to do.

I know, because I have lived far too many years under the weight, shame, and guilt of a decision I made. A choice that I know – without a doubt – that I'm forgiven for, thanks to Jesus' finished work on the cross. But it's taken me years to forgive myself.

I had an abortion.

There, I said it. I ended a pregnancy, on purpose. I made a choice to kill my baby. Writing this now with tears running down my face, I am transported back to that time. I was a divorced, single mother with a 7-year-old. How could I have another baby? My daughter was living with her aunt at the time – while I stayed with a friend, sleeping on her couch in a very small studio apartment. I was in a financial mess. How could I bring another baby into the world? I'd only known the baby's father for a few months. I met him through a friend, and while he seemed to have it all together, what did I know? He told me he was divorced and had a daughter as well. I found out later that he was still married. I was beyond terrified; I was scared to death.

What do you do when you find yourself in a hopeless situation entirely of your own making? I wish I could say that I cried out to the Lord and asked Him for help. I wish I could say that I knew this little baby was a blessing and that God would provide. I wish I had done a million different things except for the one thing I did. My pregnancy was not a surprise to God. He knew this little one just like He knew each one of us before we were formed in our mother's womb. (Psalm 139:13) I believe the baby was a girl. God had plans for that little girl. Just like He has plans for each of us. But God also gave us free will. We have the freedom to make decisions that align with His will. Or not.

We have the freedom to accept the gift of Jesus. Or not.

He's longing for a relationship with His children. He wants to walk with us through the valleys and disappointments of life. He wants to rejoice with us on the mountaintops. We can't earn God's love or do anything to make Him love us more... or less. We simply need to choose to accept His gift.

It's a reckless kind of love that, despite our sin, God still loves us.

The lyrics of this song say it so well:

> *Oh, the overwhelming, never-ending, reckless love of God*
> *Oh, it chases me down, fights 'til I'm found, leaves the 99*
> *And I couldn't earn it*
> *I don't deserve it, still You give yourself away*
> *Oh, the overwhelming, never-ending, reckless love of God*
> ~Reckless by Cory Asbury

We obey God because He commands us to. (Deuteronomy 30:16) As believers, our obedience not only honors God, but is a very tangible way we can acknowledge what Jesus did for us. Our actions show God how much *we* love *Him*.

I struggled with this because I really did love God. I knew He loved me too. The only way I can explain this season in my life is that I operated on autopilot. Have you ever driven somewhere, lost in your thoughts, only to arrive at your destination with no idea how you got there? I was simultaneously deep in my thoughts and just surviving. The enemy kept me in a constant state of confusion. After, I believed the lies that I was beyond redemption because of my decision to end my pregnancy.

You see, when I found myself in this valley, I finally *did* cry out to God. *Lord, what have I done? How could you still love me?* I felt so broken, shattered. I know He heard me, but I was running. Ashamed, embarrassed, full of self-doubt and guilt. How could I – a good, Christian girl who knew better – willingly disobey the Lord? I was tormented. I ran so far away from the love, grace, and forgiveness that eventually found me. But it would be years later.

How precious we are to Jesus, that he will *never* leave us. We sometimes find it hard enough that another human could love us, much less the Creator of the universe. How could God want anything to do with me, a sinner? *But, praise Jesus, He does!*

Impossible as it may seem, He will never forsake us. (John 14:18) And even if it takes months, years, or decades, God will welcome us back with open arms.

Remember the prodigal son? (Luke 15) Jesus shares a story about a farmer and his two sons. The older son was the good boy. He followed the rules and helped his dad with the farm. The other son – his younger brother – was the wild one. He asked his dad for his share of his inheritance and left home to see the world. He felt like there was more waiting for him. More of what, we can only guess. Maybe more fun. More experiences. Maybe he just needed to get away from his older brother, who he competed with his whole life. The younger brother may have felt like he could never measure up, especially to the brother that did everything right. But soon, he found himself living in a pigsty, eating slop. Humiliated, he realized he had hit rock bottom and wanted to go home. He knew he had to ask his father to forgive him, which his father willingly did. In fact, his dad was so happy that he organized a feast to celebrate the son's return.

Just like the father in this story, God forgives us. No questions asked (He already knows anyway!) We are simply forgiven.

I wish I could say that once I realized I was forgiven, life was hunky-dory. But that would be far from the truth! I ended up marrying the fellow. We went on to have a beautiful baby boy. And even though I knew I was forgiven, I still struggled with shame.

Our marriage didn't last. We divorced when my son was two. I was now a twice-divorced single mom with two children, with two different baby daddies. Can you say "statistic?"

At this point, all I had was God. This time when I cried out to the Lord, I was all ears, desperate to hear His voice. All my mistakes, all my shame, all my guilt – was just too much to carry on my own. I needed Jesus. (Matt. 11:28)

> *"For I know the plans I have for you," declares the Lord, "plans to prosper you and not to harm you, plans to give you a hope and a future."* (Jeremiah 29:11 NIV)

This scripture became my lifeline. I started reading my Bible again. God's Word came to life for me in brand new ways. I began to really understand the Good News of Jesus and what He did for me. The only way I can share this story today is through His strength. (Philippians 4:13)

I was 33 years old and felt like my life was just beginning.
I had hope.
And a future.

A part of that future involved a big move. I needed to sell my property. I was commuting to work each day, dropping off my daughter at middle school and my son, now four years old, at pre-kindergarten. It was time to move closer to the city. I was also tired of living on a dirt road that felt like a washboard every time I drove on it!

I began to pray that God would send the right person for the property, someone who would enjoy country living as I had for the past ten years. That summer, I did have two prospective buyers, but through a series of conversations, it was clear that I was "making something happen." Have you ever prayed for God's will to be done and then tried to help speed up the process? Yep, that was me. I was considering a rent-to-own scenario or owner financing, willing to lose the equity I had accumulated.

And then I remembered God's promise.
Trust Him. (Proverbs 3:5-6)

I made a decision that each day I would simply trust and obey.

I knew it was in God's plan for me to move. I just had to be patient. We all know how much fun that can be! So, while I was waiting, I also began to trust Him with my finances and started tithing and giving to my church. As a single mom, it was often a choice between groceries or gas, so this was a huge commitment! But God says, "I will open the windows of heaven for you. I will pour out a blessing so great you won't have enough room to take it in! Try it! Put me to the test!" (Malachi 3:10 NLT)

While I was praying for a buyer, I was also praying for my new home—specifically, a house with a pool and a fireplace. And enough parking for family and friends. Most city homes had small driveways, and I was used to two acres. I wanted enough parking for everyone.

Do you know that when God shows up, He will sometimes show off? After five long months, someone was interested in my house. The caveat: he had to sell his house first. "Where do you live?" I asked. He told me, and I skipped church the next day so I could go look at it!

Can you guess what happened next? His home had the pool and the fireplace. There was a giant back porch, three bedrooms, and a converted garage. AND a driveway big enough for eight cars! We ended up trading homes, and I received one of my biggest blessings. I believe my new house – *with everything I prayed for* – was God's reward for my obedience. For trusting Him during this process and taking my hands off the wheel.

Only God.
Only grace.

Also, God has a sense of humor. The city started a pavement resurfacing project in my new neighborhood the week I moved in. I would drive on a dirt road for another two months!

Sweet Sister, what the enemy meant for evil, God can truly use for good. (Gen. 50:20) He takes our mess and creates a message. A message that may be ugly and seemingly unforgiveable, but a message of forgiveness and hope.

Yes, I am 100% responsible for my choices. As we all are. But we cannot allow our past mistakes to keep us from accepting God's gift of grace. It's easy to think that our sin is too big and too much for God to forgive. We may feel like we are so far from God that we need a telescope to find Him. But He hasn't left. He is patiently waiting for us to come back home. And because of His love and grace, I know that when I get to heaven, the little girl whose life I took away here on earth will jump into my arms. And God will gently dry my tears, again.

I love what King David wrote: "Oh, what joy for those whose disobedience is forgiven, whose sin is put out of sight! Yes, what joy for those whose record the Lord has cleared of guilt, whose lives are lived in complete honesty! When I refused to confess my sin, my body wasted away, and I groaned all day long. Day and night your hand of discipline was heavy on me. My strength evaporated like water in the summer heat. Finally, I confessed all my sins to you and stopped trying to hide my guilt. I said to myself, 'I will confess my rebellion to the Lord.' And you forgave me! All my guilt is gone." (Psalm 32: 1-5 NLT)

We are forgiven.
Jesus paid the price.

His shed blood on the cross defeated the enemy for all time. The power of our testimony is mentioned in the same breath as the blood of the Lamb. (Revelation 12:11 NIV) How amazing is that? God says our testimony will defeat the enemy, but we must first be willing to share it with others. The good, the bad, and the ugly.

Maybe you're wondering:
How can God use me?

Satan would have us believe that we are too messed up, damaged, and unworthy for God to use us. But God says we are loved, chosen, and forgiven. The evangelist, Billy Graham once said: "The unbelieving world should see our testimony lived out daily because it just may point them to the Savior."

You have a message that needs to be shared. We all do. I know my story is not unique and there are many women who have overcome trials and obstacles, hidden sin, and very public mistakes. The enemy would love for us to keep our stories hidden in shame. But when we share our burdens and past sins with each other, God can use our story to strengthen and encourage others.

For so many years I felt "less than" and now I finally realize my worth in God's eyes. I pray that my story will help you see your value in His eyes too.

Sis, I know your story will shed the light of God's love into someone else's burdened-filled life. God loves you, just like He loves me, and He is calling us all "for such a time as this." (Esther 4:14)

CONQUERING INFIDELITY TO GOD

by Kimberly Ann Hobbs

The quality of being faithful in service unto God is very important, but we find in today's world that being unfaithful to what He has called us to as believers is very common. We see some who begin a work in their calling with full anticipation of charging forward and accomplishing great and mighty things, only to find that they give up in a short amount of time, allowing their light to be diminished. Please God, help that not be us.

Often, Christians on duty for Jesus somehow lose their zeal and passion over time, and they eventually leave the area God has called them to. It's very sad. How can we conquer this attitude of infidelity to God and be victorious in our mission to Him?

One way is to be cautious and not to lose the fear of God in your life. We can become unfaithful to Him when we dare to go against Him.

> *The fear of the Lord is the beginning of wisdom, and knowledge of the Holy One is understanding.* (Proverbs 9:10 NIV)

God has counted us worthy to serve Him, and He equips us with knowledge from His Word. To remain faithful to Him, we need to possess an attitude of gratitude over our calling daily. If we complain about our God-given duties in serving Him, before we know it, we will have abandoned our post and, ultimately, our God whom we serve. We must maintain a heart of thankfulness to serve God.

Be cautious not to covet earthly rewards for self-gain in being a Christ-follower.

> *Listen to the truth that I speak: whoever gives you a cup of water because you carry the name of Christ will never lose His reward.* (Mark 9:41 TPT)

> *Put your heart and soul into every activity you do, as though you are doing it for the Lord himself and not merely for others. For we know we will receive a reward, an inheritance from the Lord Yahweh, the Anointed One!* (Colossians 3:23-24 TPT)

Focus on serving God with a grateful heart to avoid the infidelity that the enemy wants you to have toward the God who loves you and the God who has called you according to His purpose.

Great is God's faithfulness to you, and may you hold the faithful post of honoring Him with your service victoriously.

. . . .

SHELLY HAAS

is originally from Northeastern Ohio but has called South Florida her home for many years. Her entire professional career was in banking. She has a heart for women's ministries and has served in a leadership role for a number of years. Shelly finds joy in seeing women study, learn, and pray together and empowering them to grow in their relationships with God. She has also been a lay minister for Cancer Support, a ministry in her church. Currently, Shelly hosts a small Bible study group in her home and also volunteers in her community at a historical museum, providing guest tours and educational tours to children. She enjoys spending time with family and friends, studying the Word, reading, and living in Florida. Additionally, Shelly loves animals and adores her calico feline friend, MeeKé.

TRUSTING IN GOD'S ULTIMATE VICTORIES

by Shelly Haas

It was Wednesday, August 26, 2015. The day began for me like any other workday. Although I had often heard of unimaginable tragedies happening to other families, I certainly was not prepared for it to be our family, not today or any day.

I grew up in Ohio with one sister and had moved to Florida in the late eighties. I loved Florida from the very first time I visited. I had wanted to move for a while, and eventually, I decided to make it a reality. Many years later, at about midday on that fateful day in 2015, I received a text from my niece that her mom, my beloved sister and only sibling, had been diagnosed with a large brain tumor through an MRI. Receiving a text with this kind of news was certainly unexpected. My wonderful niece was just 22 at the time, and she had taken her mom to the MRI appointment by herself as her dad was out of town.

Until about two weeks before this, we had only known my sister to be a healthy, active, and spiritually centered wife and mother. Without a doubt, my sister loved God, her husband, and their daughter. She loved animals, nature, the beach, had a sense of humor, an artistic talent for drawing, and a need to keep her home in perfect order at all times. She was 17 months younger than me, and we had always been very close. Even though distance separated us physically during much of our adult lives, our hearts were always very much connected, and we looked forward to our in-person visits. I called her about once a week on my commute to work so we could "catch up." But I had noticed that over the past couple of weeks our conversations had changed. That very morning she mentioned that she had a doctor's appointment that day, but she was unable to tell me the purpose of the appointment. I was not sure what was going on. I had even told a couple of my close friends about my concerns and asked them to pray. My brother-in-law and niece recently noticed that she had been having some memory issues and difficulty finding words in her conversations.

After her text to me, my niece took her mom directly to the hospital, as directed by their family doctor, and they admitted her for further testing. A family friend joined my niece at the hospital, and my brother-in-law returned home later that day. I left work that day, never to return, after a 40+ year banking career.

I felt like I was in a fog. I remember my senior pastor's wife praying with me that night on the phone...I am still so grateful for that. The prayer focused my mind, but I was still in total disbelief at what was happening. Although I knew little about what was ahead, in less than 48 hours I was on a plane to my hometown in Ohio. The fact is that I was embarking on what would become a 13-month journey of becoming a co-caregiver for my sister.

Based on the MRI, the oncologist and neurosurgeon felt my sister had glioblastoma, which we would learn is a VERY aggressive type of brain tumor. Furthermore, the location of the tumor made surgery to remove it very high risk, or probably a better way to say it is that the tumor was "inoperable." We needed a definitive answer as to what exactly we were facing, so the neurosurgeon performed a biopsy, the results of which were inconclusive. However, after doing the biopsy and despite not being sure that it was indeed glioblastoma, the doctor felt that removing the tumor would possibly be less risky than he had originally thought. We held onto this encouraging news.

We moved from our smaller town to a larger city, where we could have access to a brain tumor center of a large, well-known hospital. This move was necessary because a glioblastoma tumor is rather uncommon – only about 12,000 cases are reported in the United States annually. *(mdanderson.org)* My sister had a second biopsy, this time confirming that she did indeed have glioblastoma. The neurosurgeon told us, straightforward and bluntly, that this type of tumor normally reoccurs within a few months, even with treatment. I remember the day well. My brother-in-law and I felt totally devastated. A few days later, we met with their oncologists to learn their recommended treatment plan for my sister. They were offering the standard of care treatment: chemotherapy and radiation.

The statistics about this type of tumor were startling. The median survival rate for glioblastoma, considered a grade IV tumor, is 15-18 months. The five-year survival rate is about 10%. *(mdanderson.org)* We knew statistically that the odds were stacked against us. We were in the very beginning stages of learning about this disease, but we knew we needed something more; we needed an "out of the box" treatment. Was it in God's plan to bring my sister through this? Could she be a part of this 10% survival rate? We kept on praying and moving forward. Time was of the essence

We had faith, we believed in miracles, and we believed that God is our healer, so we armed ourselves for the fight.

> *Jesus went throughout Galilee, teaching in their synagogues, proclaiming the good news of the kingdom, and healing every disease and sickness among the people.* (Matthew 4:23 NIV)

After we had the weekend to digest everything, the first thing my brother-in-law did on Monday morning was to contact my sister's pastor and his priest and make appointments to go see both of them that day. He had such presence of mind to make that his first choice of where to turn. Then he got immediately busy researching and looking into every possible treatment option for my sister.

Then God stepped in full force. First, He provided an army of prayer warriors to cover us in constant prayer. Of course, we had the prayer, love, and support of TWO spiritual leaders and their churches. Because we are a small family, having long-standing family friends and the most incredible, amazing neighbors to come alongside us was crucial for our spiritual and emotional support. We asked them to pray. They diligently prayed and then asked for prayer from people from all walks of life. God blessed us with so much prayer for my sister to be healed and comforted. These same friends and neighbors remained with us throughout our journey, providing much-needed assistance. I received unparalleled support from friends at home. God loves us so much!

Next, God connected us with notable neuro-oncologists at Duke Cancer Center and MD Anderson Cancer Center in a way that only He could accomplish. Some good friends mentioned to my sister and brother-in-law that they had seen a segment on "60 Minutes" about some clinical research at Duke University's Preston Robert Brain Tumor Center on glioblastoma, including a procedure they were doing with some success. And my brother-in-law's associate's daughter personally knew a surgeon at MD Anderson who had spent much time researching glioblastoma. God is always working.

Now my brother-in-law had two great options to immediately research, both being among the best of the best of Cancer Centers. With the very little information that he had, the next morning he contacted Duke Cancer Center. They responded that they would get back to him within three days to let him know if my sister qualified for this treatment. We prayed that she would, even though my brother-in-law had learned that she did not meet all of the criteria. All he wanted was a chance to speak with the doctor to try to convince him to consider her case. We waited. The call did come from the doctor, who said to send in the information on my sister and they would review her case! That's all we could ask for. I was left in tears of thankfulness to God. Seeking all avenues, my brother-in-law also made contact with the doctor at MD Anderson and provided him with the biopsy results.

While we waited to hear back from both clinics, my sister was doing just okay. She was having some problems with verbalization and balance, and was getting very tired. Then, one evening after dinner, as she got up from the table, she lost her balance and fell. Fortunately, she did not hurt herself. Soon after, she could no longer walk the short distance from the family room to the bathroom or go up and down the stairs without assistance. She could no longer be left alone. We quickly put plans into play to accommodate necessary changes to their home. We borrowed a wheelchair from friends, which we would put many miles on during our journey. How was everything changing so fast? And, we had not heard back from either of the Cancer Centers.

We had a long weekend, but on Monday we received the call from Duke Cancer Center. They gave us an appointment for the following Monday to meet with their team and to evaluate and make their recommendations for a treatment plan for my sister. And... if she was eligible to be accepted to any of their clinical trials, we would need to meet with them again on Tuesday. We prayed for the Tuesday meeting. My brother-in-law and I cried so many tears of happiness. This was the opportunity we had been asking God to grant us.

My sister's ability to function continued to steadily decline. She needed our help with just about everything; even some everyday tasks were becoming difficult. The doctors said it was because of the tumor's growth. Meanwhile, my brother-in-law procured an appointment at MD Anderson, whose neuro-surgeon believed that the percentages of success for removing the tumor were better than we had been told. This gave us renewed optimism, but then again, could he be over-promising?

With all of these challenges and unknowns before us, the three of us left on Sunday morning to drive to Durham, North Carolina, to the Duke Brain Tumor Center ahead of our scheduled Monday morning appointment. Upon meeting the doctor, who had credentials and research experience beyond anything we could have ever imagined, we immediately saw her genuine compassion. Seeing my sister's condition, she was truly concerned with making her comfortable. Although my sister did not qualify for any of the clinical trials being done there at the time, the doctor made very aggressive recommendations for my sister, stating that she must not be given the standard treatment of chemotherapy and radiation together at the beginning. Instead, she would be given chemotherapy in a daily pill along with chemo infusions and a drug that would limit the blood supply to the tumor. The goal was to stall the tumor's growth and hopefully reduce it with time. The treatments would be administered locally at home, and we would travel to Duke every two months. After considering everything, we felt strongly that the recommendations made to us at Duke were the right answers, and we knew that God had brought us there. We decided on this option.

Treatments began soon after our return home. She handled the treatments with few side effects and started to regain strength. Her cognitive skills, motor skills, and verbalization were all improving. The first MRI, after four weeks, showed that the tumor was stable. The treatments were relieving the pressure on her brain. We began to eat healthier, which meant organic foods, plant-based foods, and low sugar intake. She was even able to enjoy the 170+ birthday cards she received in answer to a request made by my brother-in-law to friends and neighbors who spread the word in a really big way! I took her to art classes, and she began her love of drawing again. We felt it was important to keep her busy and keep her brain active. We were so thankful to God.

My niece accompanied her mom and dad back to Duke for her first eight-week checkup in December. My niece presented the doctor with samples of the drawings her mom had been doing; the doctor was amazed, but I am sure God was not surprised! Her most recent MRI revealed that the tumor was 35% smaller! The doctors were ecstatic, not to mention our excitement. Our prayers were being answered. The treatments continued, and at the next eight-week visit to Duke, the MRI revealed that the tumor had shrunk about 50% from its original size. God is good! She would then take a two-week rest from treatment and then begin with radiation for six weeks along with a chemo pill.

While glioblastoma itself is not painful, the effects of everything else that she was subjected to took a toll on her body. While she never complained, she was weak and fatigued. She was again having trouble with verbalization and motor skills. Blood work showed a very low platelet count, which is not unusual for chemo patients. She was given a platelet infusion, and headed off to Duke for her next checkup in April. On this trip, the scan showed very little change in the tumor size. However, further testing revealed a blood clot near her lung. She was immediately admitted to the hospital at Duke where she remained for the week before returning home. I will never forget going to the airport to pick them up and seeing her come out in the wheelchair with her arms outstretched to me.

Due to concerns of more blood clots, she now had to have injections of blood thinner twice daily in addition to the platelet infusions. All along, we remained positive and prayerful that her platelets would begin to regenerate on their own. Then in July, she fell. The injuries initially seemed to be minor, but a small abrasion became infected, which soon led to her being hospitalized again. My sister received strong antibiotics to fight the infection, which led to kidney problems and kidney dialysis. (This was a particularly hard process for me to watch her go through; it was so hard for her.) Still, her platelet count was very low, and now additionally, her white blood cell count was low, requiring blood transfusions. She spent the next nine weeks in three different hospitals fighting all of these battles. From the very beginning, my brother-in-law and I both felt strongly that we never wanted her to feel alone or afraid, and we committed that one of us would be with her at all times. Now, we certainly were not going to leave her alone in the hospital, so my brother-in-law would stay during the day, and I would come in the evening and stay at night. I am so thankful that we made that choice and God gave us both strength and health to keep our commitment.

Despite all the measures that were being taken, there were no changes in her condition, and she was being put through so much. There came a time when my brother-in-law and I, along with the advice of medical teams, had to make difficult decisions, the hardest ones of our lives. Although we had prayed for a different outcome, we had to resolve that we had done everything humanly possible and that God's ultimate plan for my sister's life was different than ours; it was so much bigger. The fight being over, the victory being His, we relinquished this precious being into God's loving care.

> *In everything give thanks; for this is the will of God in Christ Jesus for you.* (1 Thessalonians 5:18 NKJV)

My brother-in-law is an extraordinary human being. In 2015, in addition to his wife becoming ill, he lost two siblings and a sister-in-law. Yet through everything, he was strong and determined. He presented a positive outlook to my sister in everything. He never gave up hope. It was his love for God and his wife that kept him going.

Blessed is the man who trusts in the Lord, And whose hope is the Lord. (Jeremiah 17:7 NKJV)

After I returned to my home in South Florida, I realized that God's plan included a victory for Him in me as well. As I reflected and looked back, I could see God's hand in everything, and I could see His leading. God had provided the time for me to be with my sister. It was never, easy but He had given me the strength that I needed. I have always been a believer and studied the Word, and I have taken an active role in my church for many years, but this journey had strengthened and solidified His holiness, power, and love in me. It took me a while to connect all of the dots, but when I did, it brought about in me a life of total committed devotion to God. I realized, through God's grace, that I wanted to walk closer to Him and receive ALL of His blessings!

If you are going through or have been through something like I have and are struggling with the outcome, allow God to reveal His purpose for your life through reflection and prayer. When you ask God, He will always answer in His way and in His time. Be faithful with your prayers. My heart was broken, and living my life without my sister will always be hard, but I know that I can trust God and celebrate the victories He has given me. God gave me the victory of a deeper walk with Him while He gave my sister the ultimate victory - eternity with Him. The following are Scripture verses that I held close during my journey, and I claim them for you as well.

I can do all things through Christ who strengthens me. (Philippians 4:13 NKJV)

Trust in the Lord with all your heart and lean not on your own understanding. (Proverbs 3:5 NIV)

Your word is a lamp for my feet, a light on my path. (Psalm 119:105 NIV)

Conquering Control

by Kimberly Ann Hobbs

Many of us struggle with multiple things in our lives, such as worry, anger, and depression. But how many of us struggle with the desire for control?

All the way back to the garden of Eden, we see Adam and Eve's struggle with control. God said to them, "you must not eat from the tree of knowledge of good and evil." (Genesis 2:17 NIV) What did Satan do in response? Satan tried to discredit God by accusing Him of withholding good from His children. He told Eve she shouldn't trust God to define good and evil for her; but that she needed to do that for herself. Then she would have control.

Today, in pride, we still crave control. I struggled with this myself until I realized my desire for control is part of the ongoing curse of sin. Despite this, I cannot excuse my own controlling behavior and dismiss it as acceptable. No! I want to be victorious over this struggle, and acknowledging that I'm not the only woman who battles this controlling spirit helps me take it to God when it emerges so I can conquer it. And I ask the same of you. Will you take your controlling behavior to God?

The devil wants us to think that if we have control, we can make our lives better. We believe that lie and want to decide for ourselves what is best for us. But one day, we will wake up to what God says, and we will see that life does not revolve around us or our thoughts and desires, as we once believed.

Think about the enemy of our souls and how he desires to capture our hearts. He tells you that control will bring you peace, safety, power, comfort, respect, and so much more. But this is not true, and only God, in His infinite wisdom, sovereignty, and unending love, can deem what is best for us.

Dying to a desire for control is not easy. It takes a humble heart to admit this sin to God and yourself. We must recognize and admit that we are not God. We are not all-knowing or even able to make every decision in our lives. We must surrender.

Trusting God for each circumstance, relationship, and choice takes extreme courage. Overcoming our own will and surrendering to His plan is the best plan. This will bring Him glory and give Him the ability to fulfill His purpose in you. Even though you think you have the best plan for your life and try to control it, God will confirm that you don't.

> *For I know that good itself does not dwell in me, that is, in my sinful nature. For I have the desire to do what is good, but I cannot carry it out.* (Romans 7:18 NIV)

As you surrender control to God, remember to pray and seek Him first before making any decision and be comforted knowing what He says in Isaiah 55:8-9 NIV:

> *"For my thoughts are not your thoughts, neither are your ways my ways," declares the Lord. "As the heavens are higher than the earth, so are my ways higher than your ways and my thoughts than your thoughts."*

Pray about relinquishing all control to God and conquering the spirit of control by the power at work within you, Ephesians 3:20. Be assured that He knows what He is doing, and watch as the big things you seek to control become little in the hands of God. And victory will soon be yours for the taking.

. . . .

KRISTA FRANTZ

is a fraternal twin, dog mom to Nora, and "auntie" to many. She grew up in a small town in eastern Pennsylvania before making a move to Florida fourteen years ago. She has a passion for children and is dedicated to stewarding the next generation through time spent, conversations, and mentorship. A former public school teacher and current full-time nanny, Krista spends most of her days caring for the little ones of local families.

A true believer in the power of struggle and victory, Krista is also passionate about the importance of sharing our stories and glorifying God through them. She enjoys being outdoors, having a great cup of coffee, and challenging herself to learn new things. In her free time, she also focuses on public speaking, serving at her church, and spending as much time with friends and family as she can. Krista currently resides in Jupiter, Florida.

RENAMED

By Krista Frantz

I remember the darkness most of all - an uncomfortable blanket surrounding me on all sides, encouraging fear and an elevated heart rate. Alone I sat, trying my hardest to avoid the scary story being written in my head and the multiple pieces of old gum stuck to the bench I was sitting on. With my coworker long gone, I dialed home for the second time. The answering machine picked up, kindly reminding me that although it respected my efforts, I would again hear no familiar voice on the other end of the ringtone. Twenty minutes late. They were never late. Maybe it was the lingering sugar high from the countless samples snuck during my shift or possibly the confidence I had in them up to this point, but I remained hopeful. Any minute, the headlights of our 1995 Dodge Neon would round the back of the building, Mom or Dad in the driver's seat. They would apologize for being late, check that I was okay, and we would spend the short ride home talking about my oh-so-eventful evening, a sophomore in high school, working at the local ice cream shop.

Except that moment never came. Ten more minutes, then ten more. No headlights. No Mom or Dad. No work conversation. At some point between being intimidated by my exclusivity in the darkness and a legitimate concern for my parents' well-being, I made the decision to move from the bench. My feet hit the concrete and almost immediately held an energetic pace. I would've preferred them to stay in the parking lot of the shop, but the darkness, fear, and insecurity I felt on the outside bench kept me company the entirety of my twenty-minute walk home.

Twenty minutes. It doesn't seem like a whole lot of time - just enough time to run through the Starbucks drive-through on a Saturday morning, clean the floors of my now apartment, or read a few pages of a C.S. Lewis novel. But if you've ever sat with your thoughts for twenty whole minutes, you may understand what I experienced that night. A plethora of self-created and severely inaccurate storylines and conclusions surrounding the explanation of what actually happened formed all too quickly, and felt more real than the event itself. Some time in the duration of my walk, similar to each ice cream flavor that I spent hours serving to customers that night, I created labels. Except these labels weren't ones that could be painstakingly peeled off the glass, changed, and replaced with little effort. No. These labels, like tattoos, imprinted themselves far past the surface and, although uninvited, would selfishly make themselves comfortable for decades to follow. These labels, unqualified and relatively unsubstantiated, attached themselves aggressively to who I believed I was. Forgotten. Abandoned. Rejected.

. . . .

There's something about this next story. Although, I can't tell you what that is. Yet. I have a vague memory of it being fall. I am not sure it was. It could surely be the temperature of the memory rather than the season itself, but let's go with it. We found ourselves on a quiet, narrow road somewhere off the main one. With little to say and even less understanding of what awaited us, I sat silently, eyes peeled to my surroundings, trying to piece together the puzzle. I deemed myself a "master of puzzles" at this point, commonly searching for meaning and piecing together limited knowledge in a desperate attempt to comprehend the events that were taking place around me. I had become a spectator (and a puzzle master) in a story that, I felt, was no longer mine.

A basketball court enclosed with high, metal fencing, maybe even some barbed wire. A structure resembling a quite casually constructed mobile home, light yellow in color, revealed itself as our final destination. Bleak and desolate, our souls seemed to carry an ironic reflection. With the car in park and our hearts in neutral, we exited the car, jackets and brave faces in hand. Somewhere between the front door and the hallway that followed it, we were told I would have to wait in the car. Minors were not allowed. As mom and dad shared apologies, I took a few steps back to the car. I climbed in the backseat and sat. And sat. Unlike the last memory, I felt safe. Bored, but safe. Eventually, after some time spent listening to Christian radio and accidentally setting off the car alarm, we were all three back in the car. As Dad drove us in the opposite direction down the narrow road somewhere off the main one, I recounted the experience. It wasn't entirely terrible, considering the circumstances, minus the car alarm incident. That was embarrassing. But as I sat listening to the hum of the tires and the heaviness of silence, more labels invited themselves in the back seat with me. This time, adding to the ones that previously existed. Left out. Second best. Alone.

. . . .

At this point, I think it's fair - and necessary - to provide some background. I'll begin by intentionally communicating how very fortunate I've been from birth until now to have incredible, loving parents, who provide for me, care for me, and intercede in prayer for me always. I have never been neglected or felt like I didn't have what I needed. They sacrificed, scrambled, and sought the Lord passionately and with determination to ensure that what they couldn't provide during the traumatic struggle, He would. I am completely aware of what a privilege this is and am forever grateful for their faith, strength, and resilience.

My sister was an addict. The stories above are just glimpses into what those years looked like for me and our family. Twins, we were twelve when the enemy put his hands on her life, twenty-five when the blood-pierced ones of Jesus took over for her. Praise God for His faithfulness, His love, and the sacrifice of His Son on the cross! Thirteen years is a long time, and the chains of addiction are strong ones. Throughout those years, labels birthed out of my experiences progressively held more weight and gained momentum as I settled on the idea that I came second in comparison to her and that it made sense that way. That conclusion led to mishandled relationships, people-pleasing, and more pain. I carried burdens I was never meant to carry and held roles I was never meant to hold.

Remember the search for "something" in the second story I shared? I think maybe the "something" is truly that it seems like nothing at all. It doesn't include much of a plot and certainly not a tense or anticipated climax. The story seems pretty insignificant, actually. But part of the battle against the lying labels of the enemy is understanding who he is and what he intends to accomplish in our lives. And if I've learned anything about our adversary, it's that his meddling in the minor produces outcomes that are major.

The Bible calls the devil "a father of lies." It actually says that "when he lies, he speaks in his native language." (John 8:44 NIV) His native language; his communicative weapon of choice. It also tells us in 1 Peter 5:8 (NIV) to "be alert and of sober mind. Your enemy the devil prowls around like a roaring lion looking for someone to devour." John 10:10 (NIV) is clear that "the thief comes only to steal and kill and destroy." Liar. Manipulator. Deceiver. Thief. Accuser. Ruler of Darkness. These are just a few of the names he carries with pride.

Let me be clear. The devil has been after your soul from the moment you were created. He is on a mission to steal from you, kill you, and destroy you. He wants to tear you down, distract you and derail your purpose. Like a true enemy, he is calculated and highly motivated. Nothing is off-limits, no mercy. And I believe one of the attack strategies that tops his list is to assign us a misconstrued, inaccurately constructed, and completely perverse identity.

But, my friends, our stories don't have to end there. And I am eternally grateful that mine didn't. There is hope. I have one more story for you. This one is my favorite.

. . . .

Fast forward with me from adolescence into adulthood. Past the awkward braces stage, the learning how to best survive college stage, and the figuring out what real life is like in my first real job stage. My twenties met me, like an overlooked sliding glass door, with unexpected pain. Some of which I positioned myself to receive and some of which I did not. Either way, pain is pain. Do you know who likes to weave their way into pain? Labels.

This story, although my favorite, is a messy one. And I'm so grateful that because of God's boundless grace, love, and forgiveness, I don't have to carry the weight and shame of it. Ever.

When I was twenty-one, I met and dated a man who treasured me. I knew this because he put me before himself, laughed at all my funny (and not-so-funny) jokes, and gave me a glimpse of what human grace looks like. He was the son of a youth pastor, prioritized making others laugh, and his heart came alive when serving people less fortunate than himself. When I was twenty-two, he asked if I would be his wife, and I responded with an exuberant "yes." We spent a year planning our wedding, and when I was twenty-three, we said, "I do." The months following our "I do's" were filled with all the gifts that came with living life beside my person, but they were also filled with the harsh reality of understanding what and who we said "I do" to. The problem? Neither one of us knew who the other truly was. The bigger problem? Neither one of us knew who we were outside of the inaccurate labels we currently carried.

Within our first year of marriage, we experienced job loss, job change, loneliness within our marriage, arguments the neighbors could surely hear, disappointment in ourselves and each other, marital neglect, and betrayal. In our second year, we added intentional verbal abuse, physical altercations (this was extremely rare, but it happened), loss of hope, and disregard for the covenant we made before God. When I was twenty-five, we stood in the courtroom and declared "irreconcilable differences." Our marriage was over. More labels. Failure. Liar. Inadequate.

As you were reading, you may have been tempted to sympathize with me. I appreciate that, but I'll respectfully encourage a correction. Although a relationship involves two people, it's important to know that I acted in ways I will never be proud of, but I will always share honestly. Selfish, self-centered, and self-seeking, I entered my marriage with ignorance, looking for what was to gain rather than what I could give. Bound and carrying the weight of my childhood, the names of forgotten, abandoned, rejected, left out, second best, and alone continued to invite their lying selves to the identity party, effortlessly becoming the life of it. I was fighting for myself as I had learned to do, but this time I had fought against the man I committed to and the God I served. I defined and accepted myself by my interpretation of experiences, trauma, and pain. I lived oblivious to the spirits of fear, rejection, insecurity, lust, and pride that held me captive. Those same spirits were progressively destroying me and, without me knowing, became the most valuable players in my decision to file for divorce – a decision I now understand the magnitude of.

The years following consisted of mistreated and failed dating relationships, ambiguity in career choices, and multiple moves; all results of the shame I built through my decisions and circumstances. The Lord was moving; He was correcting, teaching, and guiding me. He was faithful, but I was content - unaware, unwilling, and in some ways unmotivated. Thankfully, our God is extraordinary and delights in transforming a moment into something monumental. The conversation was an oppositional saturation of distrust, discouragement, and determination that surfaced after the reality of another failed relationship - one that I held high hopes for. With a disappointed heart and a bruised ego, I found Him waiting for me, anxious to hear my voice and dry my tears. He is truly the most loving Father. Those few moments of organic transparency and honest communication became my catalyst for change.

The Lord began preparing my heart and redeveloping my character. Like a farmer tilling the land, He skillfully pulled sinful habits, patterns, and beliefs up by their roots, leaving a blank, fertile canvas ready for new seeds to be sown. He patiently taught me of His character and revealed to me what His love looks like in action. During this time, I prayed three bold prayers: that God would break me, restore me, and give me a revelation. The truth of His Word invaded the broken spaces of my heart, abolished strongholds, and restored my soul. He revealed dreams and gifts hidden so deeply beneath my pain that when they surfaced, I highly debated the possibility that God and I both were a little off our rockers. But the more I sought after Him and was obedient to His promptings, the more the dreams and gifts started making sense.

Almost a year in, I ran into a revelation somewhat like the sliding glass door I mentioned earlier. He wasn't only uprooting and replanting, deconstructing and rebuilding; He was also renaming. The labels tattooed on my heart miraculously held less weight, and some disappeared altogether. In their place, godly names rooted in truth began to surface. I've learned that labels, like the ice cream flavors, can be effortlessly added or modified. They can easily be incorrect or faulty. In comparison, a name is much more permanent, definitive, and holds power. The false labels that were once attached to me were replaced. Instead, I started answering to God-inspired and God-given names.

Rejected, abandoned, forgotten, and inadequate became accepted, beloved, child of God.

> *I have loved you with an everlasting love; I have drawn you with unfailing kindness.* (Jeremiah 31:3 NIV)
>
> *See what great love the Father has lavished on us, that we should be called children of God! And that is what we are!* (John 3:1 NIV)

Second best, left out, and alone became set-apart, a masterpiece, and wonderfully made.

> *For we are God's masterpiece. He has created us anew in Christ Jesus, so we can do the good things he planned for us long ago.* (Ephesians 2:10 NLT)
>
> *I praise you, for I am fearfully and wonderfully made.* (Psalm 139:114 NIV)

Failure, not enough, and shameful became free, forgiven, and whole.

> *It is for freedom that Christ has set us free. Stand firm then, and do not let yourselves be burdened again.* (Galatians 5:1 NIV)
>
> *He himself bore our sins in his body on the cross, so that we might die to sins and live for righteousness; by his wounds you have been healed.* (1 Peter 2:24 NIV)

During my renaming, He taught me the power found in laying shame at the foot of the cross and boldly seeking His throne of grace. True freedom is birthed from surrender. When I finally relinquished my pain, past, and experiences to the One who holds it all, my shame went back to hell where it belongs. I gave myself permission to acknowledge those things but boldly and confidently rejected the labels that had attached themselves. He helped me confront my pain and its manifestations with strong courage, and I freely danced on the chains that once held me bound.

Here's something about discovering identity in Jesus: no matter who you think you are or who the enemy tries to convince you you've become, God's definition of you is true and consistent. His is the most accurate of them all, the only One that truly matters. We must search for it, uncover it, and fully accept it. When we do, our hearts beat love, our minds know freedom, and our lives exude joy. Relationships become worth pursuing for His glory, not our own. Our hearts become open to forgiveness, biblical love, and undeniable purpose. Who we are is no longer a result of what we've done, the experiences we've had, or the labels that have been put on us by ourselves or others. Instead, who we are has nothing to do with us but with the God who created us, His Son who gave His life for us, and the One who walks with us daily. There's freedom from the pressure of defining ourselves and from shame, guilt, and condemnation. Freedom from striving to be, to do, or to desperately undo. Freedom from generational bondage or destructive family patterns. In Him, we are free to stop striving, wishing, and working to become who we think we can be without Him. We can run to Him with our imperfections and bask in His perfect love, confident that the One who numbered the hairs on our heads and the stars in the sky created us uniquely for His purpose.

It takes courage to face ourselves, expose the lies of identity hiding in us, and invite God to tear off the labels. But it's a battle worth fighting, one that we've been equipped for (Joshua 1:9); arguably the most critical one. Because when you conquer the lies of identity presented by the devil, your true identity becomes a weapon instead of your stronghold, and your shared testimony becomes an undeniably powerful victory won over your past instead of hidden shame. So, who were you created to be? If you don't already know, I can't wait for you to find out.

Conquering Addictions

by Kimberly Ann Hobbs

Addictions can enslave and harm us but thank God that He gives you the power to overcome any addiction. It takes hard work, but the Bible tells us:

> *I can do everything through Christ who gives me strength.* (Philippians 4:13 NLT)

God uses the word "everything" here to make it known to us that He includes "all things." This includes all your bad habits, labels that others put upon you, and all you have settled into believing about yourself. God says, "all things."

Addictions are a bondage of the heart and body that produces immediate pleasure or relief. At one time in my life, I had an addiction so strong I knew in my heart it would mean destruction to everyone around me, including myself, if I did not break that habit or the need I so desperately depended on. I craved it. I looked for the sexual relationships of men to fill a need of loneliness that only God could fill. I became addicted to the lust and desire that rose from the pits of hell to satisfy my need to never be by myself. Unfortunately, I was lying to myself that I "needed" someone to be with, therefore suppressing the truth that all I needed was God. By suppressing truth, we disconnect from God and turn to the temporal fix.

When we become enslaved to something, we are addicted. We exchange the good God intends for us for unholy and self-ruling choices. The created thing that enslaves us, in turn, allows us to become cold to God.

How did I personally conquer this? I invited the stronger power to rule over my life. God and God alone became my dependency.

I prayed daily because, in my own power, I could master nothing. I pursued Christ with all my heart. I cried to Him and acted. I confessed my addictive thoughts as sin each time they entered my mind. I repented, which meant I turned 100% away from my addiction and addictive thoughts. You cannot go halfway - you need to totally eradicate an addiction. Get rid of it. STOP IT. Just that simple - S T O P. Your mind is a very powerful thing, and by renewing your mind in Christ Jesus every day, you can do all things through Jesus Christ, who gives you the strength.

God has given you everything you need to live a godly life. His divine power within you calls us His own. Surround yourselves with believers that can help you be accountable and free.

> *For where two or three gather in my name, there am I with them.* (Matthew 18:20 NIV)

You can be victorious over any addiction. Remember Philippians 4:13 says, "all things" but it's not you-yourself, it's God who gives you the strength. Ask Him for it.

. . . .

SUSAN
TAYLOR-REEVES

is a published author who has written children's Christian fiction, including *Return to the Garden,* which is available on Amazon. Originally from Bristol, England, Sue now lives in Brisbane Australia with her husband, Scott. They have four adult children and five beautiful grandchildren. Sue is a 'Compassionate Lifer' (gentle vegan and lover of all creation) who has a passion for animal welfare. She is particularly passionate about guinea pigs and is heavily involved in the Queensland Guinea Pig Refuge. She loves finding forever homes for guinea pigs and has even adopted two herself, Teddy and Squeaks. You can read more about Sue at www.chuckleinn.com

Encountering Peace

by Susan Taylor-Reeves

> *I sought the Lord, and he answered me;*
> *he delivered me from all my fears.*
> *Those who look to him are radiant;*
> *their faces are never covered with shame.*
> (Psalm 34:4-5 NIV)

Susan and Sharon sat on the concrete steps that led up to the back garden. The afternoon sun shone down its glorious rays warming their backs, the coolness of the stairs sending just the smallest chills up their legs.

The girls sat wondering about the fact that it had been quite some months since Sharon's tortoise Speedy had gone into hibernation, and although spring was warming the air, he still hadn't surfaced.

They agreed that they should search for Speedy. Taking up a small spade, both girls began to dig in the rich soil of the old vegetable garden, where the tortoise would hide away each year. The ground now lay desolate, stripped of its winter offerings and waiting for hands to tend the soil, ready for planting once again.

Taking it in turns to dig, gently turning the soil, Susan suddenly called out, "I've found something!" she said, smiling up at Sharon.

The girls quickly fell to their knees and carefully began to move the dirt aside with their hands, revealing a small shell. Sharon very gently lifted Speedy from his hiding place and, wiping away the dirt, expected to see his little pointed head at the entrance of the shell. But, instead, Sharon could see the light shining through the shell from the other end. Sharon looked up at Susan, the shock that stole her excited smile now quickly becoming tears.

"Oh Susan, he is... gone!" she wailed, clutching the shell to her chest.

Susan quickly moved towards Sharon and, wrapping her arm around her shoulders gently, prised the shell from her hands.

"Where is he?" Susan cried, tears welling up in her eyes as she too looked into the empty shell.

Later that evening, Susan lay in her warm bed, the softness of the sheets smooth against her skin and the weight of the blankets creating a comfort only bed can bring. She waited patiently for her mother to come and tuck her in. Around and around in her head swirled questions of confusion of the missing tortoise. When you are only five years old, a mystery like this was all-consuming.

"Where could Speedy have gone? Wouldn't he be cold without his shell? Will he come back?" Susan wondered sadly. Her thoughts suddenly turned to her friend Sharon who now had such sadness in her heart.

Finally mother arrived, bringing with her a fragrance that only a mother wore on her apron - cinnamon, strawberries, vanilla - and the slightest hint of lavender that she lovingly dabbed behind her ears.

Sitting gently on the side of the bed and tucking the blankets tightly around Susan, mother looked down with a loving smile and gently swept the fringe on Susan's forehead to one side.

"Why the sad eyes tonight, my girl?" Mother whispered.

"Well." Susan began. "Sharon and I dug up Speedy today from the old vegetable garden in her yard, and Speedy was gone. He wasn't in his shell!" Susan cried, wiping a tear that had slipped out and was now sliding down her red cheek.

"Oh, I see." Mother replied, drying the tear with her hankie.

"Do you know what happened?" Susan said, wiping her nose with the back of her hand and sniffing.

"Well, you see ... um, he died." Mother said, looking at Susan with a serious expression.

"What is that?" Susan asked curiously.

"It's when you go to sleep, and you don't wake up." Mother said very matter-of-factly. "It is what happens to people when they get old; everything gets old. It's just like going to sleep. He wouldn't have felt anything."

"Come on now, just snuggle down and go to sleep," Mother said as she kissed Susan gently on the forehead and rubbed her cheek, and then, leaving the room, she turned off the light and closed the door.

Darkness filled the room - only the smallest light from downstairs filtered through the crack under the door. Susan lay quietly in her warm bed, the softness of the sheets and the weight from the blankets still hugging her gently. Closing her eyes, she imagined that she was asleep, that she would never again wake up. Her heart began to beat faster and faster, and fear began filling her like a cold chill.

"This is what it's like to be dead!" Susan began to say inside over and over. "You never wake up again. I will never be alive again!" The fear began to overtake Susan like a cloud.

Suddenly opening her eyes and throwing the bedclothes off her shaking body, her heart continuing to race, she quickly ran to the door and turned on the light, her breathing ragged, she ran as fast as she could back to her bed.

I would love to be able to write the rest of my story through the eyes of Susan, the innocent young girl, but unfortunately, this is where her story ends.

This was my introduction to the end of life, no heaven, no happy ending, just nothingness. My fear of the dark grew out of the fear of death, which then accompanied me into adulthood. I did, however, have a wonderful childhood growing up in England. Such wonderful memories of drives in the countryside, walks in the woods on a Sunday afternoon, and wonderful weekends spent in London with my grandparents and cousins. And of course, we always had summer holidays camping near the seaside. These memories I carry with me today, but most importantly, I had and still have a loving family.

My mum gave the same explanation of death that any other mother who had no understanding of the Christian life would give. She certainly had no intention of instilling fear into her child. It was just the facts, told in a gentle way. I don't recall ever talking about it again, but I am sure we must have had the discussion again at some stage.

We eventually moved from England to Australia, quickly embracing the culture of our new home as we settled into life as Aussies. Before I knew it, I had finished school and, as we did in the 1970s, became, in my mind, an adult. I worked as a secretary during the week and partied on the weekends with all my other 'adult' friends.

On New Year's Eve, 1979, the countdown to 1980 was finally over. The lights glittered above me on the dancefloor; the room was spinning slowly as I leant against my friend to hold myself up, he too leant back. All I remember from that point was being carried out of the nightclub and being placed semiconscious on the sand dune under a huge swaying palm tree.

Unfortunately, what happened next was to change my life and send me spiraling into my own dark pit of fear and shame. At the young age of 16, I was to endure a terrifying ordeal, waking to find myself being assaulted by a group of seven young men. A young unconscious girl, taken from where she slept, without consent, stripped naked down by the water's edge, on a beach in the middle of the night. I endured six hours of humiliation before being released.

"I was underage at a nightclub partying hard." That was my mind telling me that I deserved what had happened. "I drank the alcohol, and I took the drugs." An all too familiar story! I didn't tell my parents until years later and certainly didn't go to the police. I only told my closest friend and my brother. I lived with what had happened. I would carry the experience and the damage that it caused inside of me until I could carry it no more.

I had spent most of my life living in fear of the dark, but the older I became, the deeper the anxiety grew. I found that as the sun would go down, the panic would come. I found solace in other worldly things and developed an interest in looking for comfort in an array of spiritual alternatives, which would eventually lead me to Buddhism for a short time. Nothing that I tried helped to heal the damage that was still trying to destroy me.

I finally admitted at the age of 33 that something needed to change. I wanted to find peace and become a different person, and so I went on a quest to find God, not an easy thing to do when you don't believe in God.

A few days later, quite out of the blue, my daughter came home from school and said that her violin teacher would like to have lunch with me. I thought this was a lovely invitation, but just a little unusual. Little did I know that this invitation would send me on a path to healing and discovery.

As per the invitation, the following week I enjoyed a delicious lunch accompanied by a 3-hour lesson describing how Jesus had died on the cross for my sin. My daughter's violin teacher was on a mission to lead me to repentance. I knew, however, that I was a good person and, ok, I might not have been perfect, but I was certainly no sinner!

Finally, before leaving the car, she told me that she would like to give me a piece of Scripture to think about.

> *If you, then, though you are evil, know how to give good gifts to your children, how much more will your Father in heaven give good gifts to those who ask him!* (Matthew 7:11 NIV)

This Scripture was to stay with me for quite some time. In fact, it remains with me today as a reminder of the precious gifts that my Father in heaven has given me and continues to bless me with as I ask Him.

While this Scripture penetrated my heart, I didn't continue to pursue God. But, looking back now, I see that it was the seed that had been planted.

While visiting my family on the Sunshine Coast that Christmas season, I dared to go back to that same beach where I was assaulted and face the fear that had awakened in me 18 years earlier - 18 years to the day, in fact. But instead of finding fear, I met the Creator of the Universe!! This would be my mountain top experience.

My husband and I and our two daughters drove along the coast road on our way to the shopping complex in Maroochydore. The journey was spectacular, with blue skies, the sun shining off the ocean, and the waves crashing on the shore. It was picture-perfect, but as we drove south, the closer to the place where my ordeal 18 years ago had taken place, my heart beat faster, and my hands began to sweat as I dug my nails into my palms. We rounded the corner, and there it was, in full view. I knew this was the time that I must return and face my demons. I asked my husband to pull over into the car park as I wanted to get out of the car. I told him that I needed to go over the dunes and down onto the beach, on my own.

I cannot remember walking through the car park where I was held in a van for hours or over the dunes where I had been sleeping; I just remember standing on the other side looking at the ocean. The beauty was breathtaking. The hot sand beneath my feet squeaked as I walked. I turned and looked at the dunes where I had begged for my clothes. I felt numb. It was as though the attack had happened to someone else, not to me. I felt sorry for Susan, for what she had been through, not me.

Suddenly, a loud audible voice said, "Let it all go and forgive them. Look at the beauty I have made. All that is left is the rubbish in your head. Just forgive them." I was stunned as I stood there, looking up and down the beach - just me and God. Then, unexpectedly, His forgiveness flowed through me, and I forgave my attackers. I cannot explain what happened; it was as though the forgiveness that God offered me enabled an outpouring of my forgiveness for the boys.

He did not say another word. I stood in awe of His creation and in awe of His power and ability to penetrate my heart in such a way. I suddenly felt that I was floating, that my heart was beating fast, but my heart was like a soft cloud in my chest. I ran back over the dunes, back to the car, spilling joy and excitement everywhere.

We drove to the shopping complex, and I found a phone and immediately called my mum. I had to tell her that I had forgiven them for what they did. The excitement was uncontainable. I am always grateful that I was able to bear witness - my mother was able to hold my testimony of what had happened. And although it would be five more years before she too could testify to the changing grace of God's mercy, she is my witness along with my family.

While Jesus hung on that cross at Calvary, he cried out, "Father, forgive them, for they do not know what they are doing." (Luke 23:34 NIV) He took their sin, and I forgave them theirs - no names, just young men who had too much to drink and a whole lot of peer pressure. I freed them with my forgiveness as Jesus freed me with His. True victory.

Not too long after we returned from our holiday, the lady who had planted the seed took me under her wing and patiently watered it. During these early days we would spend hours together, reading the Bible and her praying for me. But even after what I had experienced, I still questioned the validity of the Bible. Then one evening, the final evening of being on the other side of the light, I stood at the front door to say good night and I asked her one final time, how do you make yourself believe? She looked at me and she quoted James 2:19, "You believe that there is one God. Good! Even the demons believe that—and shudder." (NIV)

I was shocked - demons are real! She left me standing at the front door in absolute terror as little Susan returned!

"The demons are real," I thought. I closed the door, turned off the light, and ran to my bedroom, now petrified. That night I went to bed fearful because I finally knew, after 34 years of fearing the dark, that I did have a reason to fear.

When I woke up in the morning, my mind immediately went back to that Scripture, You believe that there is one God. Good! "Even the demons believe that—and shudder." (James 2:19 NIV)

So, if demons are real and hell is real, then Heaven and God are real. I jumped out of bed so quickly and, grabbing my Bible, I opened it and started reading. I was stunned. Suddenly, the words were alive. I believed what I was reading. I believed - it was real. The words came to life. It was no longer words on a page; it was truth.

That book and those words would become my life and my truth. The book of John is is my favourite Gospel, it is a constant reminder that the Word of God, Jesus, came to earth and lived a life, He understands what it means to be human.

> *In the beginning was the Word, and the Word was with God, and the Word was God.* (John 1:1 NIV)

As I was born again, in my beginning, God said, "Forgive them." The fear of death and darkness vanished that day and was replaced with His peace and light.

> *Peace I leave with you; my peace I give you. I do not give to you as the world gives. Do not let your hearts be troubled and do not be afraid.* (John 14:27 NIV)

Twenty five years have passed since that incredible day when my heart was opened to the Gospel of Jesus Christ and I accepted Him as my Lord and Saviour. The road has not always been easy; I have fallen and picked myself up more times than I choose to count. Jesus said "Whoever wants to be my disciple must deny themselves and take up their cross and follow me." (Matthew 16:24 NIV), this is exactly what I have done, and continue to do.

As you have read my story, my prayer is that a seed of forgiveness may be planted in your heart, watered by our Father's love and out of that love, freedom will grow not just for you but for those you have chosen to forgive.

Conquering the Fear of Death

by Julie T. Jenkins

Our view as humans on earth is extremely limited. From our earthly perspective, when people die, it appears that they cease to exist. But how can a person who has grown and developed and loved, a mind full of memories and knowledge, no longer be? And if they still exist, where do they go? Where will WE go when we die? Thankfully, there ARE things we know about death from the most trusted source of all – the Bible. And as children of God, death is a fear we can conquer as we stand in relationship with Jesus!

In John 14:1-6 (NIV), Jesus speaks words of comfort to His disciples. In chapter 13, He told his disciples that He would be leaving them to go to a place where they could not follow right away. They were fearful because they didn't want Jesus to go, and they didn't know where He was going. That sounds like so many who, today, are facing the death of a loved one. Jesus teaches, "Do not let your hearts be troubled. You believe in God; believe also in me. My Father's house has many rooms; if that were not so, would I have told you that I am going there to prepare a place for you? And if I go and prepare a place for you, I will come back and take you to be with me that you also may be where I am." (1-3)

If Jesus is preparing a place for us in heaven, we may wonder how we will get there when we close our eyes for the last time on this earth. I love the disciple Thomas because he isn't afraid to say what is really on his mind, and in this case, he verbalizes the question many of us have likely thought! "How can we know the way?" (5)

> *Jesus answered, "I am the way and the truth and the life. No one comes to the Father except through me."* (John 14:6 NIV)

When we have a relationship with Jesus, He will assure our safe passage, guiding us to the home that He has been preparing for us! And what Jesus prepares will be magnificent! When you feel the fear of death creep up on you, saturate yourself in the teachings of the Bible and ask God to fill you with His peace! If you are His child, you can be assured that He has conquered death, and in doing so, allows you to conquer the fear of death!

If you have not yet surrendered your life to Christ, I invite you to pray this prayer:

Dear Jesus, Son of the Most Holy God –

I am here today to give my heart to you. Thank you for dying a sinner's death that I might live. I confess that I have lived my life without you, and now I hold out my hands to accept your gift of grace and mercy. Help me to walk in your will and your way all the days of my life. Thank you for granting me eternal life with you and replacing my fear of death with your peace that surpasses all understanding. Amen!

. . . .

CONNIE VAN HORN

is an ordinary person whom God spared and gave new life. She is passionate about sharing her story in hopes that God will use it to change lives. Connie wants the whole world to know about her amazing and loving God. She understands that we are all called to share in the mission of taking the gospel of Jesus Christ to the ends of the earth.

Connie resides in Winston-Salem, North Carolina, and attends Calvary Baptist Church, where she has participated in discipleship classes and taught Sunday school to international students. She has also attended Bible classes at Vintage Bible College.

Being a mother is by far Connie's greatest accomplishment and first best ministry. She dreams of changing the world by sharing Jesus and raising world-changers who have a kingdom perspective.

She enjoys being active in her community, making bracelets, journaling, and spending most of her time with her family. Connie wants her readers to know that it's ok to be broken - it's in our broken place that we find God. See past messy, see past broken, and you might just see a miracle.

CHASING BUTTERFLIES

by Connie A. Van Horn

If you are like me, you are an ordinary person searching for a glimmer of hope, maybe searching for answers or anything relatable to help you feel a little less alone. It is ok to feel hopeless and alone at times. It is in this broken place that we meet God and flex our courage. I can promise you this is where you are going to find hope. Hope in the impossible. Hope in tomorrow. Hope in yourself that you are more than ordinary. You are extraordinary. Victory starts by believing in yourself, and maybe even in a little blue butterfly. I hope that you will be blessed by hearing a piece of my story. It does not matter who you are or where you come from - God loves and treasures you.

When I was a little girl, I would pretend that I was someplace other than the place of my reality. I was raised in a broken environment by two broken people. My parents had four children by the time they were 22 years old, even as they were still dealing with their own childhood trauma. Meanwhile, they were actually unaware of the trauma their children were experiencing.

Due to my childhood abuse and neglect, I built very tall walls. Layers and layers of these walls were buried deep inside my own heart for years to come. As a child, I learned to play a not-so-fun game I called "hide and run." I spent most of my early years hiding from who I was and running from where I had been. It was a vicious cycle, preventing me from gaining a sense of self or self-worth, but at the same time, it was a form of protection. I thought if people never uncovered the ugly secrets that I was hiding, I would be ok. Safe.

I was gifted with imagination at a young age. I did not know it at the time, but God had given me that gift long before I had met Him. This would end up being my source of survival. I spent a lot of time hiding during my childhood. Hiding in closets, under beds, or just in general. My favorite place to hide was in a park near my home. It backed up to a river that connected to the ocean nearby. It was so peaceful and calm, and always lacked the presence of people. There, I could escape into my own, made-up world. I loved to sit against a cement wall that was down near the water. I would daydream with my eyes open, envisioning a peaceful world. I was happy and peaceful. I felt acceptance. Today, I can look back and see that God was right there holding my hand. He never left my side. He knew I would have to endure hard things, but He gave me built-in courage to survive it. He saw my future and that one day I could release hope into the world as only a broken vessel can. It's like God places you somewhere and stands with you as you grow stronger from the experience while ensuring that you do not become completely broken from it. I went through hard things, but God was there to catch my tears and pick me up when I had no strength. There is something amazing that happens to a person when they can survive any sort of trauma. I call it "built-in courage." It is a gift from God that is our sustaining source of hope and strength during hard things. And my childhood was full of hard things. But God always took care of me.

> Have I not commanded you? Be strong and courageous. Do not be afraid; do not be discouraged, for the Lord your God will be with you wherever you go. (Joshua 1:9, NIV)

God sent me an angel during those early years to offer retreat and solace. She lived somewhat close to us, and I can remember several times being thrown into her car in the middle of the night. She was kind and very warm to touch. I loved her hugs and sitting on her lap. I can still close my eyes and smell the scents from her sweaty neck and dirty shirt. My brain refuses to allow her memory to fade. I loved being wrapped in her arms. Safe. Her home is now what we would call "the projects." I did not use that term as a child. To me, it felt like a castle, and I was the princess. The walls and the flooring were made of the same brick cement. Our feet would turn completely black from the dirty floor, and I am quite sure it lacked central heat and air. This was Florida. It was hot. I slept with a big fan blowing directly on me. The roaches covered every part of the kitchen. These little critters lived happily and seamlessly with the rest of the house. I loved being at this place. I could hide from my life. I found rest, and I felt loved. God protected me there. But the devil still lurked. It was not until I became an adult that I learned that, while I was sleeping on the couch, my younger sister was being hurt in the next room. I often ask myself how our experiences at this same house could be so different.

My own home was chaotic – that's why I needed the escape. I can still hear the gunshots as the police entered our home searching for drugs. I was upstairs. I remember hiding in a closet with my mom and siblings. I was so scared. Trembling. My baby sister was downstairs, sitting next to my dad in her baby chair. My memory of this day comes and goes in fragments, but the walls built out of sheer terror were everlasting. I remember being carried out by a stranger and seeing my parents face down outside in the yard. We were sent to live in a foster home where I spent most days in a dark room, surrounded by the cries of my siblings, as we each occupied our own separate cribs. I cried too. I was so scared. Mama Betty was her name. I do not remember her being particularly mean to us, but she certainly was not warm and comforting. My oldest sister was the same age as her daughter, so she was permitted outside of the crib room to play with her daughter. The rest of us spent long hours in the crib beds. My parents continued the losing battle of keeping our family together. The fights got bigger, and the walls got higher.

When I was about six, my parents finally separated for good. We moved around with my mom from place to place. Nothing ever felt stable. My siblings and I were around constant alcohol abuse. The drinking in our home and around us was unimaginable. The fighting and yelling were a never-ending event. A burning memory came during a camping trip with a man we hardly knew. This man was a stranger and a professional con artist. He made my mom believe he loved us and enjoyed spending time with our family, and he took my siblings and me on our first camping trip. It was scorching hot in the tent. My little sister and I slept at the back of the tent, and my brother and older sister slept at the opening with the man. We did not explore the area or have any sort of fun adventure; instead, we drove to the woods and slept in his nasty tent. My little sister and I were crying and begging to leave. We were terrified. The sweat was rolling off our tiny bodies from the plastic material being pressed against us as the man yelled at us to go to sleep. Then, he threatened to hit us with his metal baseball bat. I tried so hard to stop crying. I wanted to go home. Boom... he hit me right in the side of the head. I placed my hands over my mouth as hard as I could, gripping my sister. Hot and scared, I finally fell asleep. I did not know it at the time, but the man had a premeditated plan for that night. That night, the man hurt my big sister.

After the camping trip, we moved again. And again. And again. I did not mind all the moving around from place to place. It was each move that gave me a glimmer of hope for a new life. Besides, we always packed the bags about the same time the bullies would kick it up a notch. I thoroughly enjoyed leaving them behind. But I never gained a sense of self. I walked around feeling lost, all the while fake smiling at the world. I never felt like I belonged to anyone or anything. I turned to all the wrong things of this world to fill me up, only to come up empty every single time. I hit the same wall over and over.

Running and hiding. I tried to blend with crowds hoping they would not see all my broken pieces. I hid myself and the scars so well that the true part of me just faded more and more with each passing day.

Around the time I was entering middle school, I went to live with my dad in another state. He had a very abusive woman and her children living in our home too. I tried so hard to find my place in this new world. It was not possible. My walls were too high. The pressure to fit became unbearable. I spent most school days hiding in empty stalls around the campus. My high school experience was no different. Just more places to hide.

So, at 18 years old, I set out for Hollywood, chasing anything outside of what I had known. Looking for my escape. I was going to "be something." That is where my worth settled. I needed to accomplish something great or to be great to find my worth. Turns out, I was still running. I did not stay in California exceptionally long. God was already on the move in my life, and He had other plans. My early twenties consisted of trial and error, lots of mistakes, and growth. My life at this point was just a big mess of broken pieces. And just when I thought I could not take another step, God showed up, and the greatest adventure of my life began. God was going to take this broken girl to extraordinary places. See past messy, see past broken, and you might just see a miracle.

I was in so much pain, and I couldn't see a way out. I knew something in my life needed to change, but how? I only knew broken. I had no college education, nor family, money, or resources. I was alone, and I was scared. The lies kept pouring into my heart. Useless and broken. I soon found myself living in a Quality Inn. I did not understand God's plan at the time, but I was "being still." Growing. The miracle in my story is the events leading up to my salvation and the evidence that God was already at work in my life and in me. I now realize that God used the hard thing I went through to draw me to Him.

After suffering through that period in my life, God sent me help. I was rescued from that pit and placed in another. Although this new pit was much better, it still came with its own challenges. I was living in a shelter with multiple women, sharing a home with perfect strangers, which was a great place to kill off fear and anxiety, and it worked. Clever God. It was during my time in the shelter that my life completely transformed.

The shelter was a Christian ministry with God-reminders all around. The worldly distractions were removed from my everyday life. Smart move, God. After attending church for a few weeks, I visited the pastor. We talked about being saved, but at that time, I really didn't understand what that meant. I thought I had to fix myself first. I was not good enough to be a Christian. But I had it all wrong. Broken things can become blessed things if we let God do the mending. He changes us. A few more weeks went by, and I had another visit with the pastor. That day I decided it was time; it was time for a change. That day was the first day of my "new life."

After I got saved, I was still going through hard things. And I was tired of struggling and feeling like I was in a pressure cooker. I knew I had to keep fighting, but I wasn't sure for what. The Bible says if you have faith the size of a mustard seed, you can move mountains. I always wondered what that meant, to "move mountains." I wanted to believe so badly in God's miracle, but I couldn't wrap my mind around it. Sometimes things are so big and so great that it is far beyond our imagination. I wanted to believe in something I could not see with my own eyes. So, I fell to my knees and looked up to something I could only trust in my heart. "Ok God, show me you are real... show me what you got." That is when God showed me butterflies! Jesus said mustard seed-sized faith can move mountains...because our faith is in God, and He can move the mountain.

It was a beautiful fall day. The weather was amazing, and I was taking a break in my car. I had the windows down, and the only noise was the birds singing and the trees blowing in the wind. Suddenly I looked up. I was amazed at the most beautiful blue butterfly sitting on my window. It just sat there in complete peace. It was not startled and gave me several minutes to observe. In that moment, something magical happened. That day I started chasing God.

God finds the most beautiful and precious way to draw us to Him. He knew that I would need that constant reminder of my new life and His love for me. He knew He would have to really woo me, and He did. He knew I was weak, and this world is tempting. He knew I would need something so sweet and powerful that would ultimately connect me to Him. At that moment, I began "Chasing Butterflies."

Only God can fill you up when everything else in this world has left you empty.

Over the next year, God continued to woo me and reveal many great miracles. I started to have a deep desire to share these miracles with others. I became hungry for God and His Word. I would read until I was so full. The Bible came alive, and the words would fly off the pages and speak to my heart. I was convicted about my own sin. I was seeing this world through different set of eyes. Everything just became clear. My heart was changing, and I was becoming a completely different person. A new creation!

> *Therefore, if anyone is in Christ, the new creation has come: The old has gone, the new is here.* (2 Corinthians 5:17, NIV)

After nine months of being in a shelter and a total of 19 months being homeless, God rescued me. He made me new and gave me a new life. I had a life I never dreamed could be possible. God did not lavish me with the finest, but

He gave me just enough to stretch my faith and keep me relying on Him. It's often during the on edge, gut-wrenching, pressure-cooking moments that our faith is stretched, and we are formed.

The miracles that God showed me are not humanly possible for man, but very possible for our God. God promised me a new life. Promises He has kept. He is amazing and powerful and mighty to save. He loves us so much, and He loved me when I could not love myself. He loved me when no one else was around to love me. He saved me from this broken world and gave me life. We can chase miracles in our life today if we look outside of what the world tells us to believe. Be still and quiet your noisy soul. Your answer is blowing in the wind.

> *For the Lord God is a sun and a shield; the Lord bestows favor and honor; no good thing does he withhold from those whose walk is blameless.* (Psalm 84:11, NIV)

It does not matter who you are or what you have, God loves and values you. I finally feel free from the pain that weighed me down from my childhood. It is amazing what forgiveness can become in your life when those chains are gone. Forgiveness is saying I choose to move forward in hope, peace, and love. Love is the most powerful source in the world. We can choose to love when it's hard, even when we get nothing in return, and even when it hurts like heck. It is that same love that God shows to us. The victory in my life was won through love. It is because of God's love for me that I can move forward and love others. My childhood does not define who I am. My mistakes do not define who I am. It is God who defines my true self, and it is God who decides my tomorrow. He does not care what I bring to the table. He is after my heart. God finds a heart set on Him, and He calls it out and claims it. It is not the how but rather the who. So, the next time you want to doubt yourself because you are sized up by the world, remember who God says you are. God loves you, and you are extraordinary.

Be ready to receive the miracles God is willing to send your way. I was willing and available, and I received many blessings. Now, I want to share those blessings with as many people as I can and give hope where hope is lost. The Bible tells us to go out and share with the world. God revealed Himself to me in a mighty way. He grabbed my attention and my heart. Now God says,

> *He said to them, "Go into all the world and preach the gospel to all creation."* (Mark 16:15, NIV)

Maybe the next time you see a butterfly, you will be reminded of this new life God has waiting for you. Are you open and ready for change? Ask God to reveal Himself to you.

I am like a lost butterfly blowing in the wind, chasing God, and though I cannot see Him, I know He is preparing my delicate wings for flight. God can do the impossible. Have faith and stay in the wind.

I hope by sharing my story I can be a messenger for God and a true follower of His son Jesus Christ, the One who has given all of us the grace to start over and have a new life.

CONQUERING CAPTIVITY

by Julie T. Jenkins

Captivity is not just something that happens in movies when the "good guy" gets tied up or the "bad guy" gets put in prison. Captivity is a threat in each of our lives that takes many forms.

As we examine some of the most notable instances of captivity in the Bible, we can trace that many were held captive when they turned away from God.

The Israelites were held captive for forty years, wandering in the desert even after being miraculously released from slavery in Egypt. Why? Because they refused to be obedient to God and enter the land He had given them, even voicing complaints against Him. (Numbers 14)

When Hezekiah reopened the temple in Jerusalem, he explained that the captivity of their ancestors had occurred because they had abandoned God and His dwelling place. (2 Chronicles 29)

Simon the sorcerer was held captive by his desire for power. He even offered to pay the disciples if they would impart the power that God had given them, but because of his refusal to recognize Jesus as Lord, Simon missed out on the power of the Holy Spirit. (Acts 8)

Not all captivity happens because of our own choices, however. Unfortunately, the world is filled with people held captive by sickness, financial peril, or even in abusive situations. And as many stories as there are of captivity in the Bible, there are even more stories of God's protection and release.

2 Kings 4 tells of a widow held captive by her lack of income after her husband's death. She was left with nothing except a small bottle of olive oil. Through her faith, God released her from poverty by multiplying the oil!

And Acts 16 tells my favorite story in the Bible! Paul and Silas were in prison, having been severely beaten and clamped into the stocks – and yet they chose to praise God and sing out loud! Though they were held physically captive, they didn't allow anyone to hold captive their reverence and praise to God! God noticed as they harnessed the strength that He provided, and He sent an earthquake that shook the prison, releasing Paul and Silas from physical captivity!

Threats of captivity are all around us. Yet, whether we are held captive to sin, to a circumstance due to our own actions, or are in captivity through no fault of our own, we can choose to praise God and look to Him for rescue.

Jesus is the ONLY release from ALL captivity – and when we call on Him, He will never let us down! Jesus Himself taught that He came to set the captives free. (Luke 4:18) Don't allow the devil to hold you back for one more minute from all that God has called you to. If you are trapped by fear, past mistakes, or ugly circumstances, go to Jesus. Ask Him to give you wisdom, and then take one courageous step at a time, and praise Him as you look to Him for rescue. Jesus is waiting to release you. Accept His gift as He miraculously guides you and gives you His strength to move forward to freedom. Jesus alone can conquer our captivity!

· ·

MICHELE HUGHES

Michele and her husband currently reside in Jupiter, Florida, just minutes away from the beautiful Jupiter Inlet Lighthouse & Museum. Michele's husband proposed at Marblehead Lighthouse in Ohio in 1997, and they were married the same year.

Together, they own and operate their own business, GoLifeSavers.com, which is a CPR, First Aid, and Preventive Healthcare Training Company. They also serve faithfully in church wherever God leads them, helping to inspire, encourage, empower, and equip others to find love and freedom in the one-and-only true life-*saver*, Jesus Christ.

Michele has her master's degree in education, is a #1 international best-selling author in the book *Courageous Steps of Faith*, a contributing writer and photographer in *Voice of Truth* magazine, a leader in WWL, and a retired teacher of 24 years.

She enjoys sunrises, sunsets, paddleboarding, beach walking, and capturing God's creation in photos. She loves The Father, family, friends, flowers, food, and most recently, fans!

"Give LIGHT and people will find the way." ~Ella Baker

The King's Table

by Michele Hughes

Let them give thanks to the Lord for his unfailing love and his wonderful deeds for mankind, for he satisfies the thirsty and fills the hungry with good things. (Psalm 107:8-9 NIV)

Imagine the most decadent feast - abundant in *all* your favorite pleasantries or dainties, like choice meats and wine, just as the scriptures tell us in the book of Daniel. The kings ate well, and it showed. But if we want to eat and stay healthy, does that mean that this vision of dining decadently, as kings do, is off-limits?

Eating is something we sometimes do mindlessly. Have you ever had one of those moments when you sit down to watch TV, and the next thing you know, the whole bag of chips is gone? Or have you gotten a dozen donuts for the weekend, and they only lasted one day?! Maybe you ordered the fried seafood platter with friends one afternoon, the next day gathered around the fire for a wiener roast and s'mores, and the next day it's the Chinese buffet with family. We know consistent overeating is not healthy for us, but we do it anyway. I don't know about you, but I'm often tempted to overeat.

The love of food is not a sin. But, gluttony is a sin. For me, every day is a temptation and struggle to eat the right food and eat the right amount. I'm guessing I'm not the only woman out there who struggles with weight, feeling beautiful, having a healthy body image, being self-confident, and living a balanced lifestyle. Weight loss is a multi-billion dollar industry! Some women (and some men) will try almost everything to be a certain size or have the "right" look, believing that this will lead them to feel beautiful or loved, happy, confident, or secure. The world shows us one way, but the Bible shows us another way.

> *I praise you because I am fearfully and wonderfully made; your works are wonderful, I know that full well.* (Psalm 139:14 NIV)

My hope in writing this is to point every woman to Jesus when we struggle with anything that isn't of God, to remind myself and others we are not a number or size, to encourage you to strive for health and wellness, to be comfortable in your own skin, embrace your uniqueness, and remember the Serenity Prayer: God grant me the serenity to accept the things I cannot change; courage to change the things I can; and *wisdom* to know the difference.

> *Charm is deceptive, and beauty is fleeting; but a woman who fears the Lord is to be praised.* (Proverbs 31:30 NIV)

Satan knows how to get to me. He knows how to get to *all* of us. He delights in causing isolation and for me, being overweight causes me to hide, feel uncomfortable, and get depressed. An unhealthy relationship with food can affect our relationships. When we don't love ourselves, it is difficult to be loving to others. When I was younger, I often passed up invitations to the pool and lake because I didn't want to put myself in a position where others could look at my body. Now I know the foolishness of this thought process, but we don't always have *wisdom* when we are young.

When this book comes out, I will be 53 years old. I'm now half the size I used to be. I grew up with three active and athletic brothers. In our family, anyone who wanted something to eat needed to eat it before someone else would! Generally, boys can eat differently than girls, but I did my best to keep up with them. Many times after dance classes, my mom took me through the drive-through for a Frosty and fries with lots of ketchup. My family put ketchup on everything - and lots of it! And of course, the ketchup we ate had high fructose corn syrup in it. My favorite evening snack was a bowl of ice cream with chocolate syrup and crushed pretzels. You know, the salty-sweet "fix." I kept this up until I was a teen and one day reached a size 12. Even though I grew up with a family garden and parents who prepared healthy meals, I often made bad food choices.

Fast forward to being a young adult during my teaching profession. At one point, I found myself getting so tired during class that another teacher noticed and asked if I was ok. Soon after that, I was diagnosed with low thyroid. They said that was part of the reason for my weight gain. I started on medication, which helped my thyroid, but my diagnosis was a wake-up call to make behavior changes. As our bodies change, we need to change our habits.

So I started educating myself. I discovered the book *Food and Love* by Gary Smalley, which was the start of my new mindset. My hope is that by sharing my story, including my struggles and **victories**, I can help you find your **victory** in the food war!

I can do all things through Christ who strengthens me.
(Philippians 4:13- NKJV)

My excess weight didn't come off easily. I worked hard to put it on and had to work even harder to get it off. I increased my exercise and watched what I ate. During my 24 years of teaching, I developed a cycle. Due to stress at the beginning of each school year, I wouldn't eat and would lose about 10 pounds, and then I would slowly gain it back over the next nine months. This was not a healthy pattern.

For several years, we lived on 62 acres in Ohio and even raised our own chickens. I loved cooking, having family dinners, and eating good, healthy food. Then we moved to Mississippi. The southern fried food was not my style, so I got into cooking. I was feeling "good" because my weight was at an all-time low, but even at a size 4, I still couldn't get rid of cellulite on my legs – no matter what I did. As a result, I was very self-conscious and wouldn't show my legs.

Ten years later, we moved to Florida into a small townhouse with a small kitchen. There were many great restaurants, and we loved the vibe and eating outdoors. Every day was like a vacation. The next thing I knew, within a year, I had gained 10-20 pounds. I felt fabulous but realized I needed to stop and think about what was happening in this new phase of life. Let's face it, it's hard to keep things in check while eating out a lot and enjoying beverages like cocktails, beer, and wine due to nice weather. On top of it all, we were frequently traveling, so I wasn't in my regular workout routine or habits. My size 6 was starting to get tight. So, the "party" stopped, and I got back into my regular habits: workouts, eating more whole foods and eating out less, drinking more water and fewer "beverages." And *wallah* – my body started changing, and I was getting healthier. AND we were saving money.

If you're like me, you hang onto clothes of various sizes because, as women, it is common to fluctuate in weight. So I hung onto those size 12 clothes for years because I figured one day I'd need them again, and I thought having them gave me *security*. However, soon it was over ten years that I had remained a size 6, but I still wouldn't wear shorts.

If you've ever been to Florida, then you've seen all the "beautiful people" who live and visit here. It's easy to feel intimidated. But, I soon realized we all have issues. And I also realized that I wanted to enjoy the outdoors and the beach. That was my moment of freedom! I decided to get rid of all my "big girl clothes," determined never to need them again. And I bought some shorts! I know that I'll never have long, toned legs, but I *can* maintain my weight and focus on being healthy. I decided that I won't hide and miss out anymore on invitations, relationships, and life.

Several years later, the 50's hit. Hormones changed me again - hot flashes began, and all those "wonderful" repercussions of going through "the change of life." It was time for *another* behavior change to keep things in check.

Taste and see that the Lord is good; blessed is the one who takes refuge in him. (Psalm 34:8 NIV)

For most of us, from the moment we are born, food gets shoved in our mouths. When we cry, we get food. When we are sad, we eat. When we are tired or bored, we eat. Breakfast, lunch, dinner, and snacks - EAT, EAT, EAT! And for a lot of us, food rules our life - *we live to eat*! For many of us, food is readily accessible and plentiful. We often use it for good behavior; we bribe people with it and use it as a reward or punishment. Food is often the center of holidays, birthdays, and other life events. Then, one day, we find ourselves unhappy, in pain, depressed, overweight, and maybe even sick. We may find it very challenging, almost impossible, to reverse years of habits.

Some causes of weight struggle include genetics, attitude, upbringing, society, disability, lack of knowledge and self-control, addictions, unresolved issues, body types, disease, lack of exercise, injury, hours spent driving or in front of a computer, or even lockdown during a pandemic. Some of these things we can control, and others we can't. But if we look at our lifestyles honestly, we would probably all find ways to improve the treatment of the temple that God has given us.

My husband and I recently participated in 21 Days of Prayer & Fasting with our church family by following The Daniel Fast. This was the deepest and most committed fast we've ever done. The Daniel Fast consists of eating only fruits and vegetables and drinking only water. Even though we did lose some weight, the true benefit was the intimacy we gained with God and how He moved and spoke in my life through my obedience.

Do you think that eating only fruits and veggies and drinking only water would cause you to lose weight? Of course! But Daniel didn't! He fasted not to lose weight but to be obedient to God. And in the process, Daniel trusted that God would care for his body as he was obedient to Him. You see, Daniel and his three friends were in training to become part of the king's court, and one of the aspects of that training was that they would be served meals of the best quality so that they could become even healthier and stronger than they were. But Daniel asked to not be served those rich foods so that he would not defile himself and compromise his faith. The attendant was hesitant because if the young men in his care lost weight, the attendant himself would be beheaded. So they struck a compromise. Daniel and his friends would eat only vegetables and water for ten days. The result was that these young men, in their obedience to God, actually gained weight and became fatter in flesh. A miracle took place. Only God could have supernaturally provided for Daniel. We, too, can trust that God, our provider, will care for us as we are obedient to Him.

> *Blessed are those who hunger and thirst for righteousness, for they will be filled.* (Matthew 5:6 NIV)

After following the Daniel Fast for the 21 Days of Prayer and Fasting, my husband and I noticed how good we felt; and we had gained *wisdom*. We asked ourselves, "Knowing what we know, why would we go back to our old ways?" Will we ever eat things like dessert, meat, and chips again? Yes, but now we eat them less often. Although we have eliminated some specific foods, the biggest difference is that now we are more educated about the consequences of different foods. The enemy comes to steal, kill, and destroy. He has tried using food as one of those weapons, and many of us fall into the trap, often resulting in disease, addictions, even death. We can't prevent death, but we can do our part to live a better quality of life while living by trying to prevent illness. God will reward our obedience. The Daniel Fast awakened us to a new truth. We can't expect God to heal what we allow Satan to steal.

There is so much information available about what we should eat, not eat, when, and how to eat. It is all a bit confusing and overwhelming. It's hard to know which diet is best. I see the word *die* in diet and the word *life* in lifestyle. We must each educate ourselves, listen to our bodies, and be in tune with the Holy Spirit through prayer and Bible study. It isn't selfish to take care of yourself. It is a command.

So, what *does* the Bible have to say about what we should eat? One of the most important things it says is that we are to honor our bodies and treat them well.

> *Do you not know that your bodies are temples of the Holy Spirit, who is in you, whom you have received from God? You are not your own; you were bought with a price. Therefore, honour God with your bodies. Although this verse is written as a guide to sexual sin, we can not miss the fact that Paul speaks of the body as a temple, and Christians should abstain from anything that defiles the temple so we can draw closer to Christ and become more like Him.* (1 Corinthians 6:19-20 NIV)

A good friend of mine learned I was writing this chapter and told me I needed to read *The Maker's Diet* by Jordan S. Rubin. She said I would love it, and she was right. The back cover says, "Are you looking for a health plan that is biblically based and scientifically proven? *The Maker's Diet* is just that. Using a truly holistic approach to health, this groundbreaking book leads you on a journey that will change your life."

Rubin emphasizes the importance of whole foods, walking, exercise, deep breathing, positive thoughts, music, water, honey, prayer, meditating on God's Word, laughing, and reducing stress. His summary is, "Don't worry! Fast and be happy!" I don't know about you, but this sounds like the **best** plan to me!

> *I lift up my eyes to the mountains - where does my help come from? My help comes from the Lord, the Maker of heaven and earth.* (Psalm 121:1-2 NIV)

Treating our bodies well, doing "all the right things," won't prevent death and disease, but doing our part is the best form of prevention. I am passionate about health and wellness, and I am passionate about our Creator. He made everything we need, and He allows us to choose a better quality of life for ourselves. Remember, wellness isn't just what we eat or not eat. We all want to look good, right? But ultimately, don't we want to feel good? Are you waiting to reach a certain size or weight to feel happy? Healthy looks different on different people. Skinny doesn't equal healthy. The heart determines your health. Can you perform certain tasks? Do you get short of breath after the first flight of stairs? Are you getting enough rest?

> *Happy is a man who finds wisdom and who acquires understanding.* (Proverbs 3:13 CSB)

My husband and I own our own business, Go Life Savers, LLC. It is a CPR, First Aid, and Preventive Healthcare Training Company. We see and know the damaging and even deadly effects of heart disease. According to the American Heart Association, "heart disease and stroke are leading causes of death and disability in the U.S." Heart diseases remain the No. 1 killer of all Americans. (heart.org, 2021.) Have you heard the saying, "You are what you eat?" This is truer than many want to believe. We have taken this to *heart* and choose to combine all our passions into our lives: business, ministry, personal, and professional.

> *So whether you eat or drink or whatever you do, do it all for the glory of God.* (1 Corinthians 10:31 NIV)

Although your journey may look different from mine, I'm sure you can relate to some of this. As women, our bodies go through many changes. Therefore, we need to change along with it. The struggle **is** real. I try to focus on wellness in *spirit, mind,* and *body* and to embrace the results. It's not about perfection but progress. For me, change started with a desire, and **victory** continues through education, transforming the mind, prayer, fasting, and the spirit of self-control. If and when you do "indulge," do it slowly and enjoy it. My grandma used to say; "The first bite tastes the same as the last but looks different on the body."

> *Then Jesus declared, "I am the bread of life. Whoever comes to me will never go hungry, whoever believes in me will never be thirsty."* (John 6:35 NIV)

> *Why spend money on what is not bread, and your labor on what does not satisfy? Listen, listen to me, and eat what is good, and you will delight in the richest of fare.* (Isaiah 55:2 NIV)

Who doesn't love gathering around a table with family and friends sharing a good meal?! The dinner table was and still can be the time where people share and develop relationships. We have all been invited to eat at **The King's** table forever. And although we will enjoy many choice delicacies at His table, the best part will be the company!

> *Yet to all who received him, to those who believed in his name, he gave the right to become children of God* (John 1:12 NIV)

There is room at the table. Come.

> *Dear friend, I pray that you may enjoy good health and that all may go well with you, even as your soul is getting along well.* (3 John 1:2 NIV)

CONQUERING TEMPTATION

by Julie T. Jenkins

Temptation! That's a pesky yet familiar word! Wikipedia describes temptation as "a desire to engage in short-term urges for enjoyment that threatens long-term goals." Temptation can be innocuous or life-threatening, and the devil can trick us into believing that a temptation may not be quite as disastrous as we choose to think. That's what happened in the Garden of Eden.

In Genesis 1:29 it is recorded that God gave Adam every fruit tree for food. So far, so good. As long as we can have what we want without stipulation, we are fine, right? This fruit was *pleasing to the eye and good for food.* (Gen 2:9 NIV) Even better! Adam could have whatever he wanted, and it all looked really good!

And the Lord God commanded the man, "You are free to eat from any tree in the garden; but you must not eat from the tree of the knowledge of good and evil, for when you eat from it you will certainly die." (Gen 2:16-17 NIV) Uh-oh. Temptation enters the scene. But dying? That's a pretty high price to pay for a piece of fruit, especially when it all looked delicious. Certainly not worth it.

So it seems like Adam was okay for a while. He kept busy. God had things for him to do! He had to name all the animals and the birds. And then God made Eve, and Adam had to name her. And I'm sure there was more to do between the two of them!

Enter the serpent, who connivingly befriends Eve, making her feel like it was "normal" to hang out with a talking snake. That should have been a clue.

Tip #1: Be careful who you hang out with!

The serpent asks, *"Did God really say, 'You must not eat from any tree in the garden'?" (Gen 3:1 NIV)* Notice Eve's response: *"We may eat fruit from the trees in the garden, but God did say, 'You must not eat fruit from the tree that is in the middle of the garden, and you must not touch it, or you will die.'"* (Gen 3:2-3 NIV)

Ummm...not exactly. God didn't say they couldn't touch the fruit, only that they couldn't eat it.

Tip #2: Know the facts!

Eve could have asked God. When we don't have all the facts, we can ask God, too, in prayer and by reading His Word.

> *"You will not certainly die," the serpent said to the woman. "For God knows that when you eat from it your eyes will be opened, and you will be like God, knowing good and evil." (Gen 3:5 NIV)*

Tip #3: The devil always lies!

The devil convinced Eve that the cost of the temptation was not as high as she first thought and that it would be worth it. And then the game was over. He won as she took the first bite. How often do you and I fall into that same trap? And how many times are we going to listen to the devil's twisted words, telling us what we *should* believe, which is too often the same as what we *want* to believe? How can we conquer temptation?

Tip #4: We must go to God before temptation strikes!

When we go to God and ask Him to prepare us with His wisdom and His strength, He WILL equip us to conquer temptation. I encourage you to read and pray the Psalms! Here are a few to get you going.

In you, Lord, I have taken refuge;
   let me never be put to shame;
      deliver me in your righteousness. (Psalm 31:1 NIV)

Answer me quickly, Lord;
   my spirit fails. (Psalm 143:7 NIV)

I trust in you;
   do not let me be put to shame. (Psalm 25:2 NIV)

Temptation is not new, but it is a tried and true trick of the devil, and it is not easy to stand against. But God knows the ropes even better than the devil, and He will empower you to conquer temptation - if you let Him.

ARLENE SALAS

is a Christ follower, a greeter at her church, devoted wife to Angel (whom she has known for over 37 years), mom to Valerie and Fabian (her handsome son-in-law), and grandmother to two beautiful granddaughters. Arlene works in account receivables at a hospital and is a district leader for her own financial services business. She enjoys educating others to take control of their finances and equipping them with the tools they need to succeed! She loves helping people.

Arlene was born and raised in New Jersey. She later moved to South Florida and still resides there. She loves spending time with her family and beautiful granddaughters and reading the Bible and other books that inspire her to improve herself.

Arlene is on the leader's team at Women World Leaders ministry, which was the catalyst for stepping into her God-given purpose and opening her own business.

ABANDONMENT & REJECTION

by Arlene Salas

My story is one of God's triumphs over human abandonment and rejection.

It began when my father and mother divorced when I was just three years old. I know that adult relationships are more complicated than a three-year-old can understand, but what I understood then was that my father left to begin a life with a new family, causing me, my brothers, and my mom so much pain. Many years later, I can now pronounce that God brought victory even through the pain and the tears. To God be all the glory!

> *They triumphed over him by the blood of the Lamb and by the word of their testimony; they did not love their lives so much as to shrink from death.* (Revelations 12:11 NIV)

My father met his future wife (and future ex-wife) while my parents were still married. When he left to begin his new life, my mother was left alone to raise my three older brothers and me. We lived in New Jersey. After the divorce, I saw my father maybe every other weekend for the first few years, until he moved to Puerto Rico with his new family. After that, we seldom communicated.

The little girl inside of me was missing a relationship with her father. I do not know what it is like to go to a 'Father & Daughter Dance,' and we never celebrated any holidays or birthdays together after he left. I remember going to see him in Puerto Rico when I was 12 or 13. But even after that, I still did not have much communication with him. None of us did. I could not understand how a father could be okay without speaking to his children on a regular basis. I thought, *My father and my mom divorced, but why did he divorce his children?*

My father and his new wife had four children of their own. I remember feeling sad and left out seeing his relationship with his other children from his second marriage. I felt as if I were not part of the family, and I would ask myself, *How can this possibly be? My brothers and I were born before they were.* I felt I had been robbed. I remember saying to myself, *All I ever wanted is what his new family has.*

My mother remarried when I was 12, and, unfortunately, it was not a healthy relationship. Her husband was an alcoholic at the time. He always drank at the bars and was verbally abusive to my mother when he was drunk. After 15 years of marriage, they divorced. Once again, I was disappointed. Two failed marriages. My mother has always been such a good woman who worked hard to take care of her four children. She never received child support, and she was our mother and our father. All I can ever remember was my mom working extremely hard, at times two jobs, to support her family. I adore and admire her so much for always giving us what she could. I am so thankful, grateful, and blessed to have her as my mother.

At the age of 13, I met the love of my life. Thirty-seven years later, we are still together. Praise God! But it was not an easy and healthy relationship at the beginning. I was very jealous and insecure. I came into this relationship broken, and yet I had no idea why at the time. I was afraid that my husband, like my father, would abandon me. I was also angry but never understood why I was the way I was. But now I know why I had always been so insecure, jealous, and felt I had no worth. At the age of 17½, I got pregnant with our beautiful daughter. I had no idea how to be a parent at such a young age. But God guided me with His mercy and grace. Now we have two beautiful children - a daughter and a son. I learned from my parents' broken marriages that I never wanted to be a divorcee. I wanted my children to grow up with their dad. I wanted to break the chains and curses in my family and not allow the sins of my parents to be passed down to the 3rd and 4th generation, as Exodus 34:7 states. I have learned that we inherit generational choices and curses. The choices made by our parents and ancestors, and even ourselves, will affect our future and our children's future.

> *Maintaining love to thousands, and forgiving wickedness, rebellion and sin. Yet he does not leave the guilty unpunished; he punishes the children and their children for the sin of the parents to the third and fourth generation.* (Exodus 34:7 NIV)

I thank God that my husband and I had a good relationship with each other after we both had a relationship with Jesus. But that didn't erase the heartache I endured growing up. At times, even as an adult, it hurt to see my father's relationship with his other children. I often felt like he loved his "new family" more, which I know now is not true but is a lie from Satan. I know my father loves all his children, and he is sorry for the pain he caused me and my brothers and mother.

My abandonment and rejection issues from my childhood made me take things to heart, often causing me to feel rejected by both friends and family as an adult. I always wanted to be liked by everyone, and I cared what others thought about me. Before having a relationship with Jesus, I remember hurting so much due to other people's actions. At times I felt so unloved and unappreciated. I often wondered why I would get treated a particular way. I was always nice and kind to others, so I felt that I did not deserve to be treated poorly. I resented others for not treating me well, and then I got upset at myself for allowing them to make me feel unworthy.

> *God created mankind in his own image, in the image of God he created them; male and female he created them.* (Genesis 1:27 NIV)

Some of the challenges I experienced later in my adult life were anger, trusting others and having low self-esteem, not believing I could achieve great things, feeling very insecure and emotionally unhealthy, and, at times, feeling unworthy.

I was also depressed at different times, which I didn't realize until I was in my early 30's. I was just sad a lot and was not interested in doing much besides working a full-time job and taking care of my children and home. I didn't understand why I felt the way I did. I had a great husband who was an excellent father to our two beautiful children, a brand-new home, a good job, and people in my life who I loved.

My father came to stay with me for two months after Hurricane Maria hit the island of Puerto Rico in September 2017, leaving the island without power or water. It took 11 months to restore power to Puerto Rico. That is when I first started to experience anxiety – as I listened to Satan questioning me - *Why was I taking care of my father when he had abandoned me? Why weren't his other children from his second marriage that he raised taking care of him?* Although I always forgave my father and treated him with love, kindness, and respect, I still felt the sadness I endured when he left me when I was three years old. After he returned to Puerto Rico, I cried so much at the guilt I felt for not taking advantage of the blessing God gave me to spend that quality time with my father, the father I had always desired. God had given me an opportunity to be with him, yet all I did was cry and listen to the devil torment me. I felt horrible after he left.

I never told my father how I felt, how much I missed having him around. I never wanted to hurt him; I already knew he was sorry. He had apologized to me, my brothers, and our mother. I love my father so much. He made a mistake when he was young. We all make mistakes. Who am I to judge him? I am so thankful to still have him and that I can talk to him whenever I want. We talk once or sometimes more a week. Unfortunately, I do not see him as often as I would like to as he still lives in Puerto Rico, but I did in July 2021 for a few days, and we had such a great time.

I've learned that forgiveness is so important.

Although it was sad to not have my father around much in my life, I always remembered reading the Bible verse to honor your father and mother. No matter what happened, I still had to love, respect, and honor the person God gave me to call father. Following that biblical teaching kept our relationship intact, giving me the opportunity to claim victory in forgiveness years later.

> *Honor your father and your mother, so that you may live long in the land the Lord your God is giving you.* (Exodus 20:12 NIV)

Looking back, I recognize that although life had not been easy in my teenage years and adult life, things took a turn when I started a relationship Jesus. I was born and raised Catholic. However, I didn't attend church as often as I should have, going mainly on holidays and special occasions. And I still felt lonely and empty. I felt something was missing in my life.

When I moved to Florida in 1995, I attended a Baptist Church for about a year. Baptists believe in the sanctity of the Bible. They practice baptism, believing that the person must be wholly immersed in water, which I had not done as an adult at that time.

I then went back to the Catholic church for about another two years. Then a good friend of mine, who has now passed and gone to be with the Lord, invited me to a Christian church she attended. I then attended that church for fourteen years. My family and I got baptized, and my life changed as God gave me the desire to know more about Jesus and his Word. I attended Bible studies faithfully for years, and I volunteered at the church. Then, in 2016, I was invited to another Christian church by a friend who knew I wanted something more spiritual and was longing for an even deeper relationship with Jesus. God led me to my new church home at exactly the right time in my life. It was there that God helped me through my brokenness and all my insecurities. I now know that I do not ever need to feel as if I never had a father, because God has always been with me.

I carried my issues of abandonment and rejection through my life. My heart and my home struggled after my father left. But because I rose to the calling God put in my life to forgive, I have been set free. I have learned that I do not need the approval of anyone else, because I have the approval of God.

> *I praise you because I am fearfully and wonderfully made; works are wonderful, I know that full well.* (Psalms 139:14 NIV)

When my relationship with Jesus was strengthened, I realized that it is okay if others do not want to be in my life. I learned to stop losing myself in wanting everyone to love me, no matter how much I yearned for that love. I still must constantly work on renewing my mind, my belief system, TRUSTING God, and knowing all I ever need is Him. Now I know my self-worth. He alone makes me worthy.

Because of my relationship with Jesus, I have learned that people will always disappoint us, but God never will. I thank God that I now have a good relationship with my brothers and sisters from my father's second marriage, despite the pain we all went through.

I always looked for other humans to give me what I needed, but the only one who could ever give me what I need without disappointing me is God. I only have one life to live and cannot walk around being angry, unforgiving, sad, and depressed. When I feel sadness or worry trying to creep in, all I need to do is to call on Jesus, Jesus. God is always there when we need Him.

If I had the relationship with Jesus then that I have now, I would have been spared so much pain in my life. Understanding who I am today and God's purpose and perfect will in my life is a fantastic feeling. I have learned the importance of knowing who I am, who created me, and why. God has a big purpose and plan for my life. God has also blessed me with an amazing family and friends who understand and love me unconditionally. I have also learned to go to God first, before I go to anyone else. God always understands, loves, and never judges me. And although life will always try to remind me of all the things that have deeply hurt me, God is also always there to remind me that I am not alone.

I pray for all generational curses to be broken in my family and in yours. Growing up feeling insecure and unworthy is never a good feeling. The feelings of abandonment and rejection that I felt at times still try to creep up on me. I must call on Jesus and remind myself that I am the daughter of the Almighty and the devil is a liar.

Today, I have been set free. I am victorious. I have forgiven my father and all of those who I have felt abandoned or rejected by. I am at peace. All the glory to God for His mercy, grace, and forgiveness.

> *For if you forgive other people when they sin against you, your heavenly Father will also forgive you. But if you do not forgive others their sins, your father will not forgive your sins.* (Matthew 6:14-15 NIV)

CONQUERING THE GRIP OF ANGER

by Julie T. Jenkins

Anger is a part of life. While we *should* be righteously angry at and ready to stand strong against such atrocities as abuse, neglect, and the worship of other gods, anger can also lead us to a sinful response.

We are made in the image of God, and God has emotions, including anger. We are reminded in Psalm 7:11 that "God judgeth the righteous, and God is angry with the wicked every day." (KJV) But God is perfect in His righteousness, meaning that He always handles His anger correctly. As humans with a bent toward sin, you and I must be prayerfully aware that the devil can easily use our anger to deter us from walking in God's will. And if we are not careful, anger can infiltrate our lives and infect all we say and do, causing us to become bitter, joyless, and mean.

How do we keep ourselves from being consumed by anger? Here are a few simple steps, straight from the Bible:

1) Don't allow anger to linger. When we allow anger to linger, it can become habitual.

> *"In your anger do not sin": Do not let the sun go down while you are still angry, and do not give the devil a foothold.* (Ephesians 4:27-27 NIV)

2) When angry, seek God's peace in prayer - and trust His answer.

> *I will listen to what God the Lord says; he promises peace to his people, his faithful servants – but let them not turn to folly.* (Psalm 85:8 NIV)

3) Examine the situation through God's eyes. Remember that what we see as challenging, He may mean for our growth.

> *"For I know the plans I have for you," declares the Lord, "plans to prosper you and not to harm you, plans to give you a hope and a future."* (Jeremiah 29:11 NIV)

4) Take action! Be ready to follow God's will. That may mean turning and walking away, or making a conscious effort to calm yourself and work toward a peaceful resolution.

> *Turn away from evil and do good; seek peace and pursue it.* (Psalm 34:14 NIV)
>
> *Those who plant seeds of peace will gather what is right and good.* (James 3:18 NLV)

5) Finally, if you find that you have ongoing, unhealthy anger, seek out a trusted Christian counselor who can walk with you through a process of healing. Someone with the gift of wisdom or healing may be perfectly suited and positioned to help you conquer anger.

> *Each of you should use whatever gift you have received to serve others, as faithful stewards of God's grace in its various forms.* (1 Peter 4:10 NIV)

Remember, anger itself is not sinful, but handled unwisely can hold us in its grip and lead us into sinful actions. When we obediently follow God's teaching, we can trust that He will guide us into victory, conquering anger's grip!

. . . .

LYNNE HUDSON

resides on the sunny Gold Coast, Australia and was brought up in Sydney, NSW. From a very early age, she had a love of art. With creativity as her passion, she always dreamed of becoming a professional artist. Her art career is varied, from having her own Graphic Art business to teaching Signwriting at college to running a busy art studio teaching art to adults and children.

Lynne and her husband of 35 years have a loving daughter, a talented musician living in the USA. Their life experiences include living in England for two years, where Lynne expanded her art career, and traveling Australia in a motorhome for 15 months so Lynne could paint the magnificent scenery as they met the most remarkable Aussie people.

Lynne has been a professional artist for over 40 years and continues to paint commissions for individuals. She teaches the fundamentals of art as well as courses on prophetic art. Lynne is also a published children's illustrator of many books and leads Women World Leaders Australia. Her art is featured in the WWL *Voice of Truth* magazine.

www.lynnehudson.com

GOD USES TRIALS FOR VICTORIES

by Lynne Hudson

I was born in Sydney, Australia, and was blessed with a loving mother who instilled in me her faith. I was brought up Catholic and always felt a peace sitting in the Catholic Church: the art, the smells, and the rituals gave me comfort.

I had a passion for art from a very early age, and it was my desire to be a commercial artist. God made that dream come true, but I never could have envisaged how He would take me on such an exciting and healing journey when He partnered with me to create. From the age of four, I was always creating, painting, and enjoying the simple beauty around me. I was a very shy child and wouldn't speak, so my painting was my world.

I grew up knowing there was a God but never realised the extent of how much He loved me and how I could have a personal relationship with Him until life happened in my fifties.

In 2010, I was enjoying my life with an adoring husband and a loving, talented teenage daughter - the perfect happy family. I ran a busy art studio, teaching art to 50 students a week and preparing paintings for solo exhibitions of my art. Life was full and good. At one of my classes, I played a "Hillsong" song, and one of the ladies mentioned that they played this song at her church. Only having been to Catholic churches, I thought, *Wow, that would be amazing.* So the next week, my daughter and I went along to her church. We loved it, especially my daughter, who was a musician. Little did I know that God's timing was absolutely perfect - to the day.

The following week I was called back to a breast screening clinic to discuss the mammogram I had a week earlier. They had found a lump, and I needed to have a needle biopsy to determine if it was cancer. My husband came with me to the next appointment. We waited for two hours in the waiting room, so anxiously waiting to see the doctor and hear the results of the biopsy. We were given the devastating news that it was a serious, aggressive cancer, and I needed to book into hospital the following week for surgery. I remember hearing this news in disbelief but asking question after question. How could this be happening? Everything was so perfect. So I thought.

To say that we were shocked was an understatement. My daughter and I were to go to our new church's function the next day; we still went, and I am so glad we did. The pastor on stage asked if anyone would like to give their life to Christ, and I thought, *Oh yes, I need Him more than ever right now.* I quickly raised my hand, and my daughter did as well. Only God knew how much we would need Him over the next year.

The following Monday, there I was, waiting to go into surgery, scared of the unknown, and again I kept thinking, *How could this be happening?* The lump was removed, and then my journey really began. I was told the lump was stage 3 cancer and that I should have chemotherapy and radiation to make sure that all the cancer was gone from my body. My husband and I agreed that this was the road we were to take, and then our challenging year began. Life was never to be the same. Looking back, I am amazed at how God was with me in every part of this journey. He held me, He wrapped me up in His loving arms, and I grew in my relationship with Him that I had never had before.

With my first chemotherapy, the nurse incorrectly overdosed my drugs, and I was violently ill. Welcome to chemo. How was I going to get through the next six months? I continued to be ill throughout the treatment, experiencing many side effects. I feel one of the worst side effects of this treatment is losing all your hair. As a woman, losing part of your breast then losing your glorious hair, eyelashes included, it was like my whole femineity was taken from me. I felt my whole identity had been stolen - from my looks to my career and my debilitating health.

I isolated over these months as my immune system was very fragile, but ladies from the church visited our home and administered communion. My daughter continued to go to the church, and her faith grew. This was an amazing blessing from this whole ordeal - that my daughter found her calling to be a beautifully anointed musician for the Lord and continues to bless people throughout the world today through her music. I am so thankful that God brought beauty for ashes for our family.

God put a beautiful, caring Naturopath in my life who helped me combat the side effects of chemotherapy with natural medicines. This was a divine chance - one of many.

God visited me during this time through my paintings. When I was well enough, I would stumble into my studio and paint. I felt compelled to paint the beautiful frescos of Michaelangelo's work from the Sistine Chapel. It was as though God was taking me back to my Catholic roots through these historical paintings, and it gave me a peace. I was taken to my happy place that I had as a child, where I was alone with my God and creating.

During this time, my husband suggested that I put this "new" artwork on my website. A few weeks later, I received an email from a prestigious New York art gallery, asking if they could represent me, and we spoke of me having an exhibition in New York. I was over the moon. Wow! How could this blessing come from so much pain? The year continued with the end of chemo, and then the radiation began. As I started to get my strength back, I began to create a body of artwork for the exhibition. My true goal of focusing was to get to the other side of this nightmare.

I finally achieved this massive accomplishment with this collection. However, we were financially ruined. The combination of huge medical bills and not being able to work meant we didn't have the funds to go to New York. We felt I had to put my dream of an NYC exhibit on hold. But God placed another angel in my life - a friend who had been through cancer and who insisted on helping us get to NYC. Praise God. He had a plan.

So three years later, after the start of this journey, we were on a plane to exciting New York City and my exhibition. God had turned everything around for His good. At the opening night, I told my testimony and praised God. But there was more to come. This was only the beginning of His destiny for me.

On our return, our daughter felt a calling on her life to go to Bethel Church School in Redding, California. At only nineteen years of age, she left Australia to go to Bethel's School of Supernatural Ministry. That year I went and spent Christmas with her, where my true calling was uncovered.

During chemotherapy my arm had been damaged, making it very painful for me to move it. Because it was my right arm that was compromised, it inhibited my process for painting. During the first Bethel service, I was amazed to see artists painting on stage. This was my introduction to prophetic art, and I loved it. The following day I went to Bethel's healing rooms for my arm.

When I walked into their main auditorium, I was astonished to see all the prophetic activity in the room, with musicians, dancers, children, and artists.

Ten artists were painting in a circle. One painting, in particular, caught my eye. It was a beautiful painting of a ballet dancer, which spoke to me of freedom of limbs. I was then prayed for by a group of Bethel students and a young twelve-year-old girl. The girl placed her hand on my arm, and I felt a fire go down my arm, and I was instantly healed. Praise God. I believe that my hope was stirred from the painting, and my healing was then activated by prayer. This was such a momentous moment for me. God showed me personally how He can heal through prophetic art, which stirred in me such a longing to create with my heavenly Father, to help others see His beauty and love. Seeing how God reaches down from heaven to produce with artists opened up a whole new world to me. I knew that this was my calling. My gift of art needed to be shared so others could witness the Father's heart through His brushstrokes. God speaks through the arts, bypassing all understanding as He touches lives.

I returned to Australia and began to immerse myself in prophetic painting. I learnt all I could about this God-given art and spent endless hours with God, creating with Him. Since that time, I have seen God work many miracles through prophetic art over the last seven years. Prophetic art is worship, a beautiful anointed time partnering with God to create what is on His heart. So many times, when God has given me the gift of painting with Him, He has revealed His heart through His guidance of the brushstrokes, colour, and design.

Four years ago I felt led to go to a different church, and, as I entered the church, I felt at home. As God would have it, the pastors had been praying for over a year for a prophetic artist to come to their church, and there I was. They invited me to paint live with their worship team the following week. No other church had asked me to do this. I was honoured, and a little scared as I hadn't done this before, but with the Holy Spirit's guidance, it was a wonderful experience. So this started another chapter of my art - painting live. Since then, many doors have opened, allowing me to do live painting at churches and events.

Five years after my healing at Bethel, I returned to be at their Bethel Creative Conference, and I was asked to paint on stage with the worship team. I was absolutely honoured. I had come full circle, and God had guided me so perfectly to be on every step of His journey. I am so honoured that God partners with me to show me the intimate details of His love that He has for us.

"For I know the plans I have for you," declares the Lord, "plans to prosper you and not to harm you, plans to give you hope and a future." (Jeremiah 29:11, NIV)

Often when I paint with God, He has a personal message just for me, but then another viewer will get a totally different message from Him through my art. This is His way of reaching out to His children. I have learnt from this visual art that a painting can speak volumes, sometimes far beyond what words alone can say. I have seen people in tears over my paintings, when words alone had not had an effect. God knows what each person needs to experience for breakthroughs.

I am continually amazed how God orchestrates our lives for His glory, for His daughters and sons. He uses our heavenly gifts to help others. God has opened up so much for me to see and to hear from Him. And He has given me the privilege to show others how to look through this window and develop a more intimate relationship with Him.

While teaching my prophetic art courses, I have seen and witnessed so many people's lives changed as they opened themselves up through the art process. I have seen people physically and emotionally healed as they paint their diseases, believing through this for a complete turnaround in their health. Sharing testimonies through the art has also activated the faith of many, leading to healings and more revelations about who we are in Christ.

I am so thankful that God interrupted my life to breathe His breath of life and love into every core of my being, allowing me to help others know Him through the process of painting with Him. When you open up to Him, He will show you His love in the simplest of signs. I have learnt from our Lord to release and receive from Him. It is invigorating and exciting to go on this wonderful journey with Him. Listen to His promptings and surrender. He has you. He always does.

Another part of my unexpected journey has been to have the honour of having my art in *Voice of Truth,* the bimonthly magazine produced by Women World Leaders. Not only has God used my art to reach others for His kingdom through this publication, but it has also given me the privilege of hearing testimonies from those whom God has touched through the pages of the magazine.

What gifting has God placed in you? Step out for Him, explore, and open yourself up to let Him show you what He has written in your Book of Life. Follow Him. He will never disappoint.

Then you will be empowered to discover what every holy one experiences—the great magnitude of the astonishing love of Christ in all its dimensions. How deeply intimate and far-reaching is his love! How enduring and inclusive it is! Endless love beyond measurement that transcends our understanding—this extravagant love pours into you until you are filled to overflowing with the fullness of God!

Never doubt God's mighty power to work in you and accomplish all this. He will achieve infinitely more than your greatest request, your most unbelievable dream, and exceed your wildest imagination! He will outdo them all, for his miraculous power constantly energizes you. (Ephesians 3:18-20, TPT)

God had me in His hands from a very early age of four. He put on my heart the desire to create with Him from this young age where I had felt so alone and shy, and He gave me a happy place to share with Him.

Through my teenage years to adulthood, though I struggled with the pain of shyness, art was my sanctuary, God's gift to me. I realized the depth of this when God fulfilled my desires through my prophetic art. This incredible journey that God has had me on (and there is still so much more to come) has filled me with a strong longing to strive to fulfill His plans, to reach my full potential as a daughter of the King. I am so grateful for this gift; I treasure it, honor it and respect it. When God reaches down from heaven to place on my heart what is burning on His heart, it is a victory for those who receive it.

God speaks to us in different ways, and I have been blessed that he uses my sanctified imagination to get His loving message across. As you spend more time with the Lord, you can't help but see His love for you.

I encourage you to use the gifts God gave you, don't waste them. We are all unique, and He uses every one of us. Know that He entrusted you with them, so develop them and partner with Him for you to shine His glory.

> *So we are convinced that every detail of our lives is continually woven together for good, for we are his lovers who have been called to fulfill his designed purpose. For he knew all about us before we were born and he destined us from the beginning to share the likeness of his Son.* (Romans 8:28-29 TPT)

Conquering the Shame of Weakness

by Julie T. Jenkins

> "My grace is sufficient for you, for my power is made perfect in weakness." Therefore I will boast all the more gladly about my weaknesses, so that Christ's power may rest on me. That is why, for Christ's sake, I delight in weaknesses, in insults, in hardships, in persecutions, in difficulties. For when I am weak, then I am strong. (2 Corinthians 12:9-10 NIV)

One of the most difficult things I find as a Christian is releasing the shame of my own weakness. I strive to do the right thing, learn, grow, and follow God in total and complete obedience. And the Bible tells us to do just that. But only God is perfect and holy, without fault and without sin, and in order to grow in all the ways listed above, we must first grow in humility, recognizing our own faults, shortcomings, and weaknesses.

Let's face it, this side of heaven, we will not be perfect. So is the correct response to cower in a corner, knowing that we can never be enough? Of course, the devil would like us to do just that! But God teaches differently. He teaches that when we recognize our weakness, we confess that He is God and we are not. And when we successfully accomplish all God calls us to *while* admitting our weakness, we put God, the true victor, on display for all to see.

Proverbs 22:4 states, "True humility and fear of the Lord lead to riches, honor, and long life." (NLT)

And Peter teaches us, "...clothe yourselves with humility toward one another, because 'God opposes the proud but shows favor to the humble.' Humble yourselves, therefore, under God's mighty hand, that he may lift you up in due time." (1 Peter 5:5-6 NIV)

You see, when we admit that we cannot "win" on our own and humbly accept God's power at work in our lives, we gain unfathomable, godly strength, joy, and peace that is beyond the understanding of our humanity. AND we put God on display in the process!

I have been married for over 25 years – and I will be the first to tell you that the success of my marriage has NOT been because I am such a good wife! And although I have an amazing husband, he is not perfect either. The fact that we are two perfectly flawed individuals with plenty of weaknesses and yet we live in a happy home and have three amazing children is a testament to God's faithfulness and goodness to all five of us! Acknowledging my own weakness, and God's blessings despite that weakness, gives me the opportunity to showcase God's goodness to a broken world.

God does not want us to be ashamed of our weakness but to recognize it, admit it, and depend on Him as we continue to grow every single day. When we are weak, that is when God's strength can be seen most clearly. And that is when He gives us a testimony that we can share – using our weakness for His glory.

· ·

Karen Burch

is an author whose works include *The Easy Healthy Cookbook, Lamby the Lullaby Lamb,* and prereading curriculum featuring historical events, illustrated by her and her family. She grew up a painfully slow reader, which enabled her to create an easier way for slow readers like herself.

She has worked in Boatwright's Family Daycare, Bethany Christian School, public school classrooms and cafeterias, and has assisted her family and neighbors in their reading development. Keys (the name Karen calls her husband because he's the provision and know-how for the calls God puts on their hearts) gave her to God like Samuel, Hannah's son, given to God. Together they watch what Jesus creates by His power: love.

Growing up through a time when riots from ethnic unrest captivated and spread in the nation, Karen learned from her parents' and sisters' examples and Sunday school the value in Thomas Reid's words, "We are only as strong as our weakest link." What do we have to hold dear if we outrun our nation's precious brothers and sisters without turning back to help those who want to rise up and walk?

Today, Karen and her husband James (Keys) are on their 3rd honeymoon as they make their home in Florida.

THE PASSOVER VICTORY

by Karen Burch

My birth brought in the year 1960. Our family lived at the base of the mountains in the San Gabriel Valley at the edge of the city of Los Angeles, California, the "City of Angels." I was a complainer. The world wasn't enough for me. I wanted the spiritual, and, at church, I gave my heart to Jesus. As I grew older, my sister and I would get up late at night to watch *The Outer Limits* and *Night Gallery*. These were fictional shows about paranormal things occurring and leaving victims in a nightmare existence. In time, I curbed my curiosity about the dark, spiritual side by turning off the shows.

At seventeen, I wasn't into dating, football, or anything an older teen aspires to be involved in. My dad said, "I can give you almost anything, but I can't give you poverty," hoping I'd understand the value of paid work. I told Jesus I believed I would make a good mom. I told Him I could adopt children and not get married. About two weeks later, I became enamored with an amazingly handsome but humble guy with kind eyes who joined the choir I was in at church. When he said hi to me, I opened my mouth to answer and drool shot out on his choir robe. He smiled. I was embarrassed. We went biking and hiking together and became great friends. While hiking back down a mountain one evening, we saw a shooting star, and both of us secretly wished to be married to each other. Sometime later, James and I were married on President's Day.

We loved our time together! Two years later, we had a baby boy. We loved having a son! This little one was a baby man! I had the privilege of being his mom. Nothing on earth could be better! James and I named him Joshua David after the leader of God's people in the promised land and a man after God's own heart. I had never had so much purpose and fulfillment as I had in a son born in the world. I knew I had found work I liked doing so much that everything else paled compared to it. I LOVED my job as a mom! One of James' dreams had been to be a young father so that he could have fun spending time with his children and they would have an enjoyable childhood.

We would spend our evenings watching our son shine in his discoveries and his practice of them. After our second son, Daniel, was born, there was more work to be done. I enjoyed teaching new things to both of them. Daniel was so calm and carefree. The two boys were true buddies. It was exciting watching them grow in knowledge, abilities, and in their responsibilities. I also cared for a friend's child during the day as we began a home daycare. Joshua received plenty of practice at leading children, and Daniel was good at entertaining them.

Neighbors of ours, who had recently moved to the United States from India, began bringing their daughter to our daycare. They always prepared Indian food for lunch, and as the mom and I became friends, the family soon welcomed our daycare children to share their lunch with them. I noticed how this family lived more like Christ than those I knew in the church, so I replaced my own church family with this extended Indian American family, and I left the church.

I also began believing in the words of the popular music of the day. One song stated, "Losing my religion." I believed this of myself. It was as if I had no free choice in the matter. It was more like a hurricane had come upon me, and I couldn't do anything about the loss of my faith in God. The Bible predicted,

"Now the Holy Spirit tells us clearly that in the last times some will turn away from the true faith; they will follow deceptive spirits and teachings that come from demons." (1 Timothy 4:1 NLT) This was me. The idea that I couldn't help losing my faith in God was purely a lie. Eventually, I pushed away the Bible saying, "It's already been fulfilled, and it's not for humanity anymore."

Over the next nine years, I developed a whole different worldview that turned my thinking upside down. The further twisting of Scripture in my mind, since I was no longer reading the Bible, led me to believe that we taught God that there is no such thing as sin, and that God and Satan had become friends and even worked together. That kind of peace and alliance was straight from the antichrist spirit, Satan, "The Father of Lies." This philosophy has spread throughout the nation under many different titles. With this foundation of deception, I began to think favorably of sorcerers and those who are grateful for Satan's works, leading me to believe that I had no enemies except Jesus Himself. The only inhibition I had was reading the Bible, which was taboo for me. This lack of truth kept me moving in a spiral heading in the wrong direction – from one seemingly cutting edge thought to another, with no Bible or Christian to ground me. I no longer believed prayer was a good thing; instead, I believed that it was just a way to order God around. I maintained that I held power through my own will that God had nothing to do with. Some evenings, James and the boys heard me scream at the top of my lungs for no visual reason. James had even seen me go into a seizure.

James told me to ask Jesus to wash my mind. This tripped me up because I believed Jesus was the imposter and everyone's true enemy on earth. I also believed that God's wisdom came through my husband to me, which, little did I know, would be my saving belief. There was an all-out war going on inside my head. Finally, I cried tears for the first time in three years and asked Jesus to wash my mind, just because James told me to. I still didn't change my mind about Jesus, but I did find myself saying things to our sons and our sons' friends once in a while that were the opposite of what I believed. There were two opposing and separate voices in my head. I began to come across people I had known from church ten years earlier, and I wondered if Jesus, the Good Shepherd, was looking for that one lost lamb - me.

During an unplanned fast, I came to my senses. I was simply poor. I had what my father couldn't give his daughters: poverty. I was poor spiritually and in all other ways. God had attended to my sister's and my mom's prayers for me. I finally saw that all of what I had been hoping for was evil, but I didn't know what the truth was. I was completely lost, and I knew it!

We drove up to James' parents' house in the country, uncertain that I'd ever come back to the city. I was scared to death that I wouldn't know how to get away from this wrong spirit I had listened to for years. For days I couldn't keep any food down. I was five feet, three inches tall, and weighed 80 pounds. One night, I closed the curtains in the bedroom and went to bed early, believing I wouldn't live through the night because I could no longer live in all of that fear. I had a heaviness on my chest like a child was sitting on it. I had served a fake god and gone the wrong way. I knew I had, by my own choice, missed love for eternity. It didn't occur to me that I could ask Jesus anything at that point. I knew that I was out of time, and I was completely remorseful. I was sad I hadn't spoken up to our sons and our sons' friends to lead them in a good direction. I related to Adam in the Bible, understanding how sorry he may have been if he knew of the trouble he had brought upon all of creation when he sinned. I was regretful to the point of gnashing my teeth. Then, the heaviness left my chest. I was so peaceful that I drifted off to sleep.

I woke up the next morning. I was alive! The first thing I did was ask James if he would take us to church. He said yes. His friend had been asking him to go to church with him for two weeks, so he had an idea of which church to attend.

I asked Jesus to come into my heart, forgive me of all my sins, including my former ill will against Him. I asked Him to make me pure. He did. We went to church, and the Holy Spirit renewed my mind through the worship songs and the preaching. The Bible was as vast as the ocean to me, and I didn't know where to begin. James told me to read John and Romans. I did. That is where I found the truth, which gave me direction. An amazing friendship resumed between me and my Heavenly Father, God. I asked my sister at Christmas, "You prayed for me, didn't you?" She nodded yes. I pictured the heaviness on my chest that one dark night as a demon. I could imagine my Savior on a white horse kicking it off of me even while I was too ignorant to call out to Him. He, Jesus, replaced that demon with "...the peace of God, which surpasses all understanding..." (from Philippians 4:7 NKJV)

Four months later, on the first day of Passover 1996, I drove over to the school to pick up Joshua. He often walked home, so it would be a real surprise to him for me to show up, especially with his tall cousin, Craig, who was in the car with me. We were on the other side of the street from Josh when he caught sight of us. Being so excited to see us, he stepped off the curb to come to us just when a car was coming from the other direction. The car had no time to stop. I couldn't help yelling to him, but I knew it would only make him look at me instead of the oncoming car, so while in a living nightmare, I rolled up my window, hoping he wouldn't focus on me. He looked at the oncoming car at the last moment and leaped up. The car struck him. The impact placed him face down on the car's hood, and he slid back off and fell in a heap onto the street. I parked the car at the curb and ran to him; the traffic had stopped in its tracks.

Josh tried to stand up to get out of the street, away from the cars, but his leg wouldn't hold his weight, and he collapsed back onto the pavement. I sat down in the street with him as he laid back. Even though his pants were covering his leg, I could see that the lower part of it bumped up in an area that wasn't his knee. I was seeing his broken leg. His face was bloody, and his pant leg quickly became blood-soaked.

The paramedics arrived and took Josh to the hospital with a split lip and a severed bone in his leg. When we were able to talk a little, one of his comments stood out: he said that two boys from his school had already died that year, one of them from a car accident. What a tragedy! Immediately I thought, *My first-born son didn't die because the blood of the Lamb, Jesus, is upon our household now!* I had just been wondering on the drive over what I would do to remember the Passover with my family that night. I had read in the Bible that Moses told the children of God to remember the Passover with a feast forever. "And this day shall be unto you for a memorial; and ye shall keep it a feast to the LORD throughout your generations; ye shall keep it a feast by an ordinance forever." (Exodus 12:14 KJV)

James and I had rededicated our lives to God, asking Him to forgive our sins by Jesus' blood on the cross, sacrificed in our place, and now we had experienced a real-life Passover. I had always related the phrase "Lamb of God" as an endearing term for Jesus as God's "little Lamb." Joshua's accident showed me a much deeper meaning to the phrase, "The Lamb of God." My husband and I had walked through God's door, Jesus. "I am the door. If anyone enters by Me, he will be saved, and will go in and out and find pasture." (John 10:9 NKJV) When Jesus died on the cross, His blood was on the top of Himself (his head) and on the sides (each of His hands), and a hyssop branch with sour wine was put up to His lips.

Foretelling this event, God instructed the Israelites on the first Passover to use a hyssop branch to put a lamb's blood on their doors to protect their first-born sons from death. "Then take a bundle of hyssop branches and dip it into the blood. Brush the hyssop across the top and sides of the doorframes of your houses. And no one may go out through the door until morning." (Exodus 12:22 NLT)

Jesus died to be the Father's Word fulfilled and our Father's Passover Lamb for us, saving us from death, saying, "It is finished." (John 19:30 NKJV)

The Heavenly Father put His own Lamb out there to the world, to save and give heavenly birth to people from every tribe and nation. John the Baptist said it like this: "The next day John saw Jesus coming toward him, and said, 'Behold! The Lamb of God who takes away the sin of the world!'" (John 1:29 NKJV) Now, because of Jesus - the Lamb of God who sacrificed Himself that our faults toward Him and each other would be forgiven - we have the opportunity to be born into the Heavenly Father's family and gain eternal life instead of death. "For whatever is born of God overcomes the world. And this is the victory that has overcome the world—our faith. Who is he who overcomes the world, but he who believes that Jesus is the Son of God?" (1 John 5:4-5 NKJV)

Josh was like one of Israel's firstborn sons on that one, dark night of the Passover. His father and I accepted that God allowed His Son to die for the release of this life-saving blood as our covering and our cleansing. The blood of this Lamb, Jesus, was the salvation of our firstborn son, Joshua, on the day of his accident.

Joshua was discharged from the hospital in a cast but James made sure he was taken to our hospital closer to home. Our doctor had new x-rays taken. They showed that the severed leg bone portions were badly misaligned. The doctor said that if the leg was left to heal in this way, one leg would be shorter than the other. He explained that this would cause Josh to have a limp, and he would likely develop spine, hip, and back problems. To correct this, he needed to remove the existing cast. After an intensive operation to align the bone with plates and screws, Joshua got up and walked out of hospitals on the third day, Easter Sunday morning.

God continued to work in our lives. I started working at a cafeteria job at the nearby school to help the family financially, and now I continue to remember Passover regularly by taking communion with other believers. "For as often as you eat this bread and drink this cup, you proclaim the Lord's death till He comes." (1 Corinthians 11:26 NKJV)

Josh went on to be a successful athlete, running cross country and competing on the track team in high school. He also joined the wrestling team and won the Junior Varsity District Championship. He graduated from the university with a degree in Aerospace Engineering. Today, Joshua is an engineer for The Boeing Company, has a family of his own, and walks without a limp.

Jesus has renewed my mind and focused me through all the former wonderings of my past to one great thought that I carry with me: God is thrilled to have a Son as much as I am; yet He lovingly spared Joshua; and just as lovingly allowed His own Son to die for us as the compassionate Lamb of God, erasing our guilt of the bad that we caused. That's the exchange, but not the end of the story. God's Son resurrected, allowing our own resurrection and conquering death for all, defeating the deceit that Satan emits against us.

> *And this is what God has testified: He has given us eternal life, and this life is in His Son. Whoever has the Son has life; whoever does not have God's Son does not have life.*
> (1 John 5:11-12 NLT)
>
> *Now since the children have flesh and blood, He too shared in their humanity, so that by His death He might destroy him who holds the power of death, that is, the devil, and free those who all their lives were held in slavery by their fear of death.*
> (Hebrews 2:14-15 BSB)

For I am convinced that neither death nor life, neither angels nor demons, neither the present nor the future, nor any powers, neither height nor depth, nor anything else in all creation, will be able to separate us from the love of God that is in Christ Jesus our Lord. (Romans 8:38-39 NIV)

CONQUERING DISTRACTIONS

by Kimberly Ann Hobbs

God has plenty to say about distractions in our life when we read His Word. The more you focus on yourself, the more distracted you will be from the proper path. God should be the captain of our ship. When we lose sight of our captain, we start steering our own vessel. We get off course as waves of sin and trials that we can't navigate on our own creep up, and missed opportunities become the norm. When our thoughts are focused on everything else but God, we miss out on the many blessings He has waiting for us in His purposed guidance.

Distraction from God can occur when we get caught up in the world's pleasures. Money, hobbies, relationships, cell phones, television, and more can all be distractions that consume our thoughts. Things we seek comfort in can be distractions used by the enemy to keep us off God's course for our life.

God tells us not to be afraid nor take comfort in the pleasures of this world. When we draw close to Him, He draws close to us.

> *But all too quickly the message is crowded out by the worries of this life, the lure of wealth, and the desire for other things, so no fruit is produced.* (Mark 4:19 NLT)

> *Do not love the world or anything in the world. If anyone loves the world, love for the Father is not in them.* (1 John 2:15 NIV)

To be victorious over distractions in our life, we must stay focused on Christ.

> *We look away from the natural realm and we fasten our attention and expectation onto Jesus who birthed faith within us and who leads us forward into faith's perfection. His example is this: because His heart was focused on the joy of knowing that you would be his, he endured the agony of the cross and conquered it in humiliation, and now sits exalted at the right hand of the throne of God!* (Hebrews 12:2 TPT)

Please prioritize your time each day and take moments for prayer. The distractions and worries of life on earth will soon vanish as moths and rust destroy them and thieves break in and steal. Store up treasures in heaven because where your treasures are, there will your heart be as well. The Bible is clear when it speaks about such things in Matthew 6:19-21.

We must never allow distractions to occupy the space where Jesus should reside in our lives.

. . . .

TINA GALLO

is an award-winning professional actress who "fully immerses herself in the character to bring life into each of her roles." She has extensive TV, Film, Commercial, and Theater credits. Tina is the only daughter of four children and is the proud mother of two wonderful sons. She toured with Frank Sinatra for two and a half years selling his merchandise during his performances. She is best known for her role as DiDi on the soap opera "General Hospital." Tina teaches acting and is the founder of 'The Nashville Studio of Method Acting.' She coaches on film sets and travels to other acting schools to speak and teach acting workshops. Tina is a leader in Woman World Leaders (WWL) and a contributing writer to *Voice of Truth* magazine. She is a lover of nature and all of God's creations, an animal advocate, and has three dogs and a horse named Journey Boy. Tina does voice-overs and is currently writing a book titled *Unfiltered, Seeing Yourself as God Sees You.*

Broken Like A Horse: My Journey from Divorce

by Tina Gallo

The spirit of a horse is broken when it is not living the life intended by its Creator. Horses were made for a purpose, and God intended people to nurture and care for them. When a horse finds itself in the hands of an uncaring or abusive owner, you will begin to see its spirit change and break down. When broken, this majestic, beautiful animal, created to be lively and exhibit strength and power, will display one of two behaviors. They will either become a restless wild soul, out of control and screaming for help, or they will become somber, exhibiting a dull expression of hopelessness in their eyes with a distant, sometimes almost lifeless countenance because their security has been shaken. A broken horse will lose trust and become less confident in its demeanor, carrying a visible uncertainty in its mannerism. Unfortunately, I witnessed this lacked confidence when my precious horse "Journey Boy" returned to me from a neglectful handler. And I witnessed this in myself when I trusted the wrong handler in my own life.

The day my spirit broke, my world shook with uncontrollable change. In an instant, the rug of love was pulled out from underneath me, leaving me in a heap of painful anguish. My husband, who I had trusted to be my rock and protector, decided for the third and final time to run away in hopes of finding someone else or something better than me. Everything internally shut down inside of me that day.

"Oh no, Lord, not again! Not again!" I cried. I was completely emotionally and physically drained with so many thoughts and questions flashing through my mind that I had no answers to. What will happen to us? I thought. What will I tell my precious little boy when he asks, "Where's Daddy?"

When my husband left, he didn't only run from me, he ran from our son, too, leaving me fearfully hanging, responsible for not only having to explain his unloving actions to our son, but also to handle our home, our finances, and my own well-being all by myself. I was terribly alone, with no one and no family around. There was only me and my son, my precious Aaron. All I could think was, What will I do now? Although he had left before, this time, somehow, I knew in my heart that he was gone for good. On that dreadful day, I saw my life pause on "stop" like a slow-motion horror scene right out of *The Twilight Zone.* Memories began rapidly flooding my mind, encircling open wounds from my childhood. This wasn't the first time someone I trusted to take care of me abandoned me. You see, my own mother left me when she gave her entire life to addictions and neglected to be present, loving, and committed. She died tragically, and young, on a bed of her sorrow, and if I am honest, a piece of me died with her. The longing for a close, loving mother-daughter relationship was robbed from me and would never be fulfilled. Abandonment by my husband echoed a voice of rewinding self-destructing lies, repeating "insecurity" over and over again. The familiar broken spirit returned as I crumbled into the depths of despair, abandoned again. The absence of my loved ones deposited rejection and inadequacy, burning and churning sharp fragments of turmoil that stabbed into every crevice of my aching heart.

"Why God?" I screamed, "Again?" A multitude of dysfunctional rotten lies flooded my being with feelings of unworthiness, rejection, pain, and shame.

These screaming insecurities intended to destroy my faith and break my spirit at its core. The enemy used weapons of abandonment and betrayal as he strategized against me, aiming to place me in a prison of unworthiness. The lie trying to repeat and imbed into my soul was a lie of deceit, enticing me to believe that I had no value, that I wasn't lovable, and that all was hopeless. Defeat screeched at me in my wounded place. You see, I wholeheartedly thought my foundation was solid in knowing that my identity and strength were in Christ. But on that day, my hope and my security in Him were threatened as I stood in a state of confusion, completely stripped down to nothing, experiencing a sense of utter helplessness as another offense of abandonment rocked my life. I wondered, *Do I really know who I am in Christ?* I pondered if I truly knew what that meant.

My heart was wounded! Fractured vessels from despair cut gaping holes deep within my soul. I couldn't believe that I was once again in what seemed like a position of utter weakness. I knew Jesus, but this resurfaced wound intimidated and confused me. There had to be more that Christ was offering me, and what I knew in confidence was that I was exhausted, and I didn't want any part of this dysfunction in my life anymore. My heart was raw and open, ferociously crying out to have its wounds healed. I began to search for the intimacy of our God's heart as I dove deep into the depths of my soul with looming questions. I had so many questions that I needed answers to and a yearning to discover what had brought me to this place. Why do I function the way I do? Why do I allow certain things? What buried hurts do I have that need uncovering to enable me to begin to learn how to heal through His Holy Spirit? How do I find that true, steady, peaceful freedom within myself that I so desire from God?

I wanted to be rid of the insecurities, strongholds, and curses that bound me. I knew that I needed to grow with God to understand these unhealed places that needed a faithful redemptive healer. The time had come for me to fully trust Him on this unfamiliar path. I needed to embrace His sovereignty so I'd be able to accept His unconditional love to learn how to live a full, prosperous life with purpose in Him. This time, with all the barriers stripped away, I decided to go on a new inward journey and take the mission road to recovery. I realized the only affirmation I really needed was from God Himself.

Looking back on the painful ploy of abandonment seeded by the adversary, I now know the reason why God allowed this second layer of destruction. It was to reopen the deep wounds of my childhood. Being pierced a second time was a work, way, and wonder of God meant to bring His intimate love and care into my life. He had plans for redemption, to fully clean out and heal my childhood abandonment pain and suffering.

Bringing a horse back from being broken takes a patient and loving handler. They must look deep into the eyes and soul of the horse and listen with understanding to gain its trust and friendship. When Journey Boy was returned to me, unsound, neglected, and confused, I knew I had to give him the space to heal. My time was devoted to him as we spent our days together, grooming, training, playing, and eventually riding again. Journey cautiously yet eagerly embraced the love that I poured into him, and every day I witnessed a little more of the return of his confidence. We bonded deeply into a fully restored, trusted relationship. Although it took some time, I never gave up on him.

As I began to heal, God never gave up on me either. He looked into my eyes and let me know that I could rely on Him. As time went by, He began to birth deep within me a desire to be free, free from the shackled lies that abandonment breathes into and onto lives afflicted by it. Welling up inside me was a daring desire to claim that I would no longer be a victim, a mere survivor who was always striving. I was going to be molded and shaped into His image by His victorious Word, obtaining the promises of my inheritance to be a strong, thriving, true overcomer, just like I had heard preached so many times and read about in the Bible. In desperation, I wanted to taste that life of true peace that was freely given to us by Jesus when He went to the cross. Therefore, I was willing to do whatever it took.

As Journey Boy healed through the passage of time, he grew stronger with a new diet and lots of exercise. His joy and will to run free returned. With new hope and excitement, he now comes running to me when I call him. For the plan to be effective, I was aware that Journey and I needed to be consistent and cooperative with one another while we worked together. In order to allow God to heal my broken spirit, I also needed to commit to a plan.

My plan of action was to first change my thought patterns and to stay closer to God than ever before. I began to meditate on the scriptures and pray continuously, reading the Bible voraciously throughout the day and attending church whenever there was a service. I guarded my heart and my mind from outside distractions, making sure to fellowship with strong, positive believers who encouraged and cared about me. A new, fiery passion to experience the fullness of God and His promises burned inside of me. With renewed hope, I was serious about surrendering every part of my life to Christ, the past, present, and future.

> *Therefore, if anyone is in Christ, the new creation has come: The old has gone, the new is here!* (2 Corinthians 5:17 NIV)

Thankfully the path to healing for Journey Boy was a straightforward one. Together, we navigated around the obstacles and setbacks that we encountered. They were mostly soundness issues with his body that needed proper care, patience, and time for his complete healing to manifest.

I encountered opposition from the setbacks on my personal path of healing from abandonment. God was my navigator, and He guided me every step of the way. Spiritual warfare brought many battles designed to steal, kill and destroy the work of deliverance and redemption during my surrendered season of inner healing. God's Spirit had quickened my heart to be prepared and cautioned me to not drop my guard again. Ephesians 6:11 tells us to put on the "full armor of God" like a heavily armed soldier so we may stand up against all the schemes and the strategies and deceits of the devil. So this time, I determined that I was going to press on with all I had to keep my mind strong and my spirit healthy to win this fight to freedom.

When trouble comes, we have a choice to either run from God and blame Him or run to Him because we know, by faith, that He is our only source. God enters into our darkness and loves us, no matter how many times we get upset, give up, or fall off the cliff. He is faithful! He promises to never leave us nor forsake us. (Hebrews 13:5)

I am thrilled to share with you that Journey Boy healed completely. He is whole, so happy, lovable, and furiously faithful. I knew as we walked through his healing that I would never leave him, but he had to learn of my love and faithfulness to him. He had to grow to trust that I was the handler that God had provided for him before he could heal completely. In the same way, I had to grow to trust God and His ways. And I can attest that God IS the perfect handler for His children.

My story of deliverance from the ashes of abandonment and God's desire to free me from shackles speaks of the great love that God has for us as His children. You see, God was faithful not to leave me with the unhealed places of my heart. He healed the rejection, insecurities, fears - you name it. His whole heart wanted me to be free, so He allowed me to be abandoned a second time, so He would truly take the place of all earthly men's influence in my life. In Scripture, we learn that if the Son sets you free, you will be free indeed. (John 8:36)

Jesus has not only redeemed my past, from my mother to the divorce, but He has truly brought me to Christ-filled freedom. He has brought me into the Holy place of His heart, transforming me into a warrior. He has given back to me what was stolen: my purpose and place under His Lordship in my life! Sometimes God allows loneliness in our lives to make room and a way for His love to enter in. I now have the God-given opportunity to serve Him daily with my whole heart through my acting, women's ministry, writing, speaking, and proclaiming His great mercy and power to all who will believe. What the enemy intended to use for evil, God used for good. Without the tenacity to overcome pain, shame, and rejection, I would never know how to deeply love, serve, and fight for the body of believers and, more importantly, how deeply loved I am. The Bible tells us that we are joint-heirs with Christ, *Now if we are children, then we are heirs—heirs of God and co-heirs with Christ, if indeed we share in his sufferings so that we may also share in His glory.* (Romans 8:17 NIV)

Through my journey of divorce, I discovered that so much of my identity was wrapped up in my husband. He became the hiding place in whom I put my confidence. With renewed faith in this new path to freedom, God taught me that I was safe in His hands and that I was fully loved as His daughter. I embraced self-esteem with a newly healed heart that my Father God restored from brokenness.

The same unconditional love and patience that God bestowed on me I imparted into my Journey Boy. Now his heart is full of love, and once again, trusting and running free like he was born to, with strong-spirited confidence.

Jesus is the true God who sees every hurting place in your life, every layer of suffering, and wants to enter in to heal and redeem them. God holds our hands through the process as we continuously connect our hearts to His. You see, the hole in my heart needed transformation. It was a polluted well that God would fill with truth, faith, belief, and trust in HIM and Him alone, no matter how dark and dismal things on this earth appeared!

People will fail us as we will also fail many, but this is true: the love of God, in whom we trust, is from everlasting to everlasting, and He will never fail us. And if we hold the love of Christ deep within us, we will be able to allow His Spirit to overcome all of our wounds, not only to clean and bandage them but to heal them, preparing us as His bride of service. We will no longer merely survive, but we will tenaciously thrive. We will see miracles flow from the places of our aching hearts that willingly surrender to Him.

Whatever ails and afflicts you, my friend, give it to Him, walk the way of complete surrender to HIM, so He can heal you and give you wings of strength to fly into your God-given destiny. *If God is for us, who can be against us?* (Romans 8:31 NIV) Now is your time, Sister! Surrender. Seek. And you will find your God of all Hosts who will fight your battles for YOU. And you will experience Victory!

Conquering Loneliness

by Kimberly Ann Hobbs

It's not uncommon to feel alone, but it's certainly not what God intended for us. Scripture tells us to draw close to God and others who will encourage us and lift our spirits in love. But often, the more we feel alone, the more we tend to isolate ourselves from groups of people, friends, or family. It's then that the enemy convinces us to slowly and painfully die from relational dehydration.

To conquer loneliness when it hits us in the face, we must settle our spirits, be still, and know and learn more about God.

Sometimes we feel rejected by the world. And even though that rejection at times is real, God is not of this world. So no matter what people may say about us or why they choose not to be around us, we can know that God is not the rest of the world, and He accepts us in His arms when we turn to Him.

> *The Lord hears His people when they call to Him for help. He rescues them from all their troubles. The Lord is close to the broken hearted; He rescues those whose spirits are crushed.* (Psalm 34:17-18 NLT)

It is obvious that many of us base part of our loneliness on faulty expectations of this life rather than fully living in the hope of the beautiful, eternal life that God promises.

We seek God first in our state of loneliness. We are also called to seek out other believers, benefitting from the encouragement that a relationship with them can bring. Look for other Christ-followers who will spur you on to Christian living. The enemy's primary purpose in encouraging us to stay isolated and alone is to distract us from God's purpose and plan in our lives.

The enemy will never guide you to spend time with those of like faith; instead, he whispers words of insufficiency into your ears. You must understand that he wants to keep you isolated and uncertain. But you are never alone because God is with you always!

God tells us, And be sure of this: I am with you always, even to the end of the age. (Matthew 28:20 NLT)

The Bible says nothing can separate us from the love of God (Romans 8:39), so no matter what the enemy whispers, YOU ARE NEVER ALONE.

Claim the promises of God to have victory over the feeling of loneliness. The beauty of being alone is that when God is all you have, you'll find He is all you need. When you are confident with His promises over you, it's only then that you will have true victory over the battle of feeling alone.

. . . .

SAMIE V. MAXINEAU

is a follower of Jesus who loves Him with her whole heart. Canadian by birth, Haïtian by blood, and American by choice, Samie now lives in Georgia. She and her husband Fred were high school sweethearts and now have three precious kids, Xander, Bella, and D'Angelo.

Samie is a Future Senior Sales Director with Mary Kay Cosmetics and has been a nationally certified Massage Therapist for over ten years. Her God-given purpose, which He has firmly placed on her heart, is to passionately serve others, which she does by using her love of self-care to minister to women and men, helping them reach for the fullness of joy of life and relationships.

Samie and her husband are also passionate about marriage and speak at marriage events sharing encouragement to other couples based on their own life experience.

She holds a Bachelor's degree in Health and Wellness and a Master's degree in Health and Wellness Coaching. Sami would love to connect with you! You can reach her on Facebook at Samy V. Maxineau.

Beautiful Surrender

By Saman V. Maxineau

The Miracle Child...

> *I praise you because I am fearfully and wonderfully made;*
> *your works are wonderful,*
> *I know that full well.*
> *My frame was not hidden from you*
> *when I was made in the secret place,*
> *when I was woven together in the depths of the earth.*
> *Your eyes saw my unformed body;*
> *all the days ordained for me were written in your book*
> *before one of them came to be.*
> (Psalm 139:14-16 NIV)

The Word of God was part of my life at a young age. In fact, my mother always reminded me that I was The Miracle Child. If not for the Word of God and the faith that she had in Christ, I would have been dead during birth. My mother was a strong warrior. I know the devil hated her and trembled every morning that she woke up. Her faith saw her through countless trials, including those with my grandmother from my dad's side. They say she was witch... well... she herself told my mother she was before she passed. My grandmother had three sons, and apparently, my dad was supposed to only have sons, but here I was. Hence the name, The Miracle Child. My grandmother tried everything she could to keep me from coming into this world. She even tried to poison my mother while she was pregnant with me, but none of it worked. Mercy said NO! My mother had a tribe of prayer warriors (Le bon Samaritain, the Good Samaritain) who came to the house every Saturday at 5 am to sing, pray, and intercede with her. She was bathed in prayers. Nothing happened to me, and growing up I got to see up close the power of God through my mother's prayers. I got to witness many miracles, which made me feel closer to God. They increased my reverence and admiration for a God who was all-powerful and all-merciful.

Misconception...

> *And my God will meet all your needs according to the riches of his glory in Christ Jesus.* (Philippians 4:19 NIV)

Many believers do not associate God with pain. At times we have all treated God as a drive-thru McDonald's. We go to Him when we want to or when we need to - misinterpreting His generosity as something we can receive at our whim. We love to place our prayer orders and expect Him to answer right away. After all, isn't He the King of kings? Shouldn't He know what we need or want before we even ask, and shouldn't He be waiting on the other side of the prayer call to grant all of our wishes? As sarcastic and harsh as this sounds, that is what many of us tend to do. And this is what I intentionally did in the year 2007.

Trials...

In August 2007, my beloved mother and best friend died of metastasis breast and bone cancer. After a long and painful battle that lasted for two years, she finally surrendered. During those two long years, the doctor misdiagnosed her with arthritis, when it was cancer eating out her bones. When mama died, I was strong at first. I even sang at her funeral when my older brother and sister could hardly control their emotions. I was calm and courageous. Some family members were happy to see me so strong, and others were confused. "She is really strong, like her mama," they said.

Was I really strong? Within a week, I became so angry at God that I could hardly pray or attend church. The more I thought about the pit that I was in, the deeper I kept on sinking. I was bitter, and being newly divorced was not helping the situation either. I was lost! *Mama prayed for people, and they got healed. Why did she die?*

Grief and Anger...

> *The Lord makes firm the steps*
>   *of the one who delights in him;*
> *though he may stumble, he will not fall,*
>   *for the Lord upholds him with his hand.*
> (Psalm 37:23-24 NIV)

A woman by the name of Lisa Nichol states in one of her coaching speeches that sometimes you have to hit rock bottom to meet the rock at the bottom. That statement was created just for me. Because In August 2007, I hit rock bottom. I began to question God, everything that I grew up believing, and even the miracles that I had witnessed.

Why, Lord?
Why could my mother pray for people, and they got healed, but she didn't get healed when she prayed or when we prayed for her?

Why, Lord?
I have seen what you could do. I have seen wonders that have blessed other people. Why didn't you do it for her? For me? For our family? Lord, she served you, she praised you, she called on you.

Why, Lord?
Why did you allow my husband to ask me for a divorce? Why did you allow everything to crumble? Lord, why have you been silent? Why did you take my mother, too...?

[Selah.]

These are some of the secret conversations that I was having with God inside my head. It was real and raw. I was bitter to the point where I stopped going to church on Sunday. Instead, I picked up extra shifts at work. The worst part of this entire ordeal is that I was going through this alone. No one knew the depth of my feelings, only that I missed both my mother and my husband. They were two of the most important people in my life, and they were both absent. I felt abandoned - as if God had forgotten about me. Despite all the lies that I was entertaining in my head, every Sunday I would feel a slight tugging deep inside my heart to surrender to God. However, I tried my best to ignore the voices whispering, "That's just not you. You are a daughter of King Jesus." The more I ignored the small voice, the gentle reminder about my identity from the Holy Spirit, the more I was troubled. I did not have any peace inside my heart. I was empty and desperately needed my Savior to rescue me, but at that point, I just could not figure out how to surrender. I was still angry at God, life, and myself for letting bitterness take root in my heart.

At work, things were fine, but it seemed like the extra money that I was earning was being drained as soon as I would earn it. I was not tithing nor supporting any congregation. THAT WAS NOT ME!! Those were not the principles that I grew up with, nor believed in. The God I served was God in good times and challenging times (at least that's what mama always said).

Redemption...

As for me, I call to God,
*   and the Lord saves me.*
Evening, morning and noon
*   I cry out in distress,*
*   and he hears my voice.*
He rescues me unharmed

> *from the battle waged against me,*
>   *even though many oppose me.*
> *God, who is enthroned from of old,*
>   *who does not change—*
> *he will hear them and humble them,*
>   *because they have no fear of God.*
> (Psalm 55:16-19 NIV)

One sunny Sunday, I was going to work and walked by my church. I could hear the church choir of Union Baptist Church. It was soothing and heavenly. As I walked to the train station, I began to cry. I could not hold it any longer. I got on the train with a heavy heart. I could not wait to get to work and let my heart pour everything out in the massage and esthetics room.

When I finally got to work and saw that my schedule was not full, I was grateful. I went to my room and cried and finally talked to Jesus! I talked to the rock at the bottom!!!

Lord, I am sorry! I am so sorry! I need you. I can't live without you. Staying away from you is miserable and unbearable. I surrender. I give it all to you. Lord, I am angry. I am sad. I am lonely. And I cannot survive without you.

Immediately after going through that cleansing session alone, I found the proper words to ask my manager for a change of schedule. That same day before my shift ended, I spoke with my manager. God gave me the words to plead with her, even knowing that there was never enough staff on Sundays. At first, she did not want to consider changing the schedule, and I expressed to her that the extra money was doing more harm than good. At that statement, she looked straight into my eyes and realized that I was desperate.

I was able to get a new schedule, and the following Sunday I was back at church, and back to Bible study on Wednesday. I was where I belonged. I was home. I asked God to forgive me and declared my love publicly to him through singing songs that I had written and dancing praise dances that I had helped choreograph.

Resolution and Praise...

Come, let us sing for joy to the Lord;
let us shout aloud to the Rock of our salvation.
Let us come before him with thanksgiving
and extol him with music and song.

For the Lord is the great God,
the great King above all gods.
In his hand are the depths of the earth,
and the mountain peaks belong to him.
The sea is his, for he made it,
and his hands formed the dry land.

Come, let us bow down in worship,
let us kneel before the Lord our Maker;
for he is our God
and we are the people of his pasture,
the flock under his care.
(Psalm 95:1-7 NIV)

Since that experience, I made up my mind that I will choose God whether or not I think He is answering my prayers. I realized that if I am with God at my lowest, then my lowest is great!! He is a good Father, not only when all is well, but also when life is rough. He is not just a drive-thru God. He is a God I can talk to. And He is quick to forgive. I learned that I don't have to hide my feelings from God because He already knows them. He just longs for me to come Him, whether I am happy or weary, heartbroken or elated. He is the God who is there when everyone else is gone.

Maybe as you read my story, you could identify relatable parts when you felt the same way - bitter, abandoned, or even angry. Maybe you feel like your world is falling apart right now. Maybe you have lost a loved one like I did. Whatever your situation might be, God knows you by name. He loves you. He cares for you and is waiting for you to run back to him. Run into His arms! He will restore you just like he did me. If you cast your cares on Him, he will renew your strength like the eagle. God wants you to depend on Him only through faith. He wants you to remember that before you were formed in your mother's womb, He knew you. You can talk to Him, cry, and share everything that you are feeling.

I am grateful for the lessons that my season of grief taught me. Now I know beyond a shadow of a doubt that no matter what comes my way, I want to be glued to the feet of Jesus. I want to stay close to Him. He is great, not because of things He can do for you and me, but because He is love, He is God, the Alpha and Omega. Our little minds cannot explain Him. He is pure. He is sovereign. We need to feed ourselves with His promises and not dwell on our own understanding. We need to affirm ourselves and remember all that He has done for us. We need to allow His words and promises to saturate us. As a result, though we will still be tempted to turn away and we will still go through trials, we will be able to pivot and not allow the devil to have free rent in our minds. Let's watch our thoughts, let's renew our minds, let's watch our actions, let's be humble, let's surrender it all to King Jesus.

I will extol the Lord at all times;
  his praise will always be on my lips.
I will glory in the Lord;
  let the afflicted hear and rejoice.
Glorify the Lord with me;
  let us exalt his name together.

I sought the Lord, and he answered me;
  he delivered me from all my fears.
Those who look to him are radiant;
  their faces are never covered with shame.
This poor man called, and the Lord heard him;
  he saved him out of all his troubles.
The angel of the Lord encamps around those who fear him,
  and he delivers them.

Taste and see that the Lord is good;
  blessed is the one who takes refuge in him.
Fear the Lord, you his holy people,
  for those who fear him lack nothing.
The lions may grow weak and hungry,
  but those who seek the Lord lack no good thing.
Come, my children, listen to me;
  I will teach you the fear of the Lord.
Whoever of you loves life
  and desires to see many good days,
keep your tongue from evil
  and your lips from telling lies.
Turn from evil and do good;
  seek peace and pursue it.

The eyes of the Lord are on the righteous,
  and his ears are attentive to their cry;
but the face of the Lord is against those who do evil,
  to blot out their name from the earth.

The righteous cry out, and the Lord hears them;
  he delivers them from all their troubles.
The Lord is close to the brokenhearted
  and saves those who are crushed in spirit.

The righteous person may have many troubles,
  but the Lord delivers him from them all;
he protects all his bones,
  not one of them will be broken.

Evil will slay the wicked;
  the foes of the righteous will be condemned.
The Lord will rescue his servants;
  no one who takes refuge in him will be condemned.
(Psalm 34 NIV)

CONQUERING PRIDE

by Kimberly Ann Hobbs

> *Your boast becomes a prophecy of future failure. The higher you lift up yourself in pride, the harder you'll fall in disgrace.* (Proverbs 16:18 TPT)

In order to conquer pride and be victorious over it, we must give God the reverence and respect that is due to Him. If we do not do this, arrogance will develop in us, and we will suffer as a result of our pride. As we study the greatness of God in the Bible, we learn of the nature of God, especially His majesty and power. Apart from God, we are nothing.

God desires you to be a loving example of His love to others. When we are prideful, it becomes an obstacle to loving others, which is one of the biblical commands.

> *For what makes a distinction between you and someone else? And what do you have that grace has not given you? And if you've received it as a gift, why do you boast as though there is something about you?* (1 Corinthians 4:7 TPT)

Self-centeredness, self-appreciation, and talking down to others identifies selfish ambition and pride in your life. God wants us to deny ourselves and be filled with grace-abounding humility. God gives us His scriptures to keep ourselves in check. In order to conquer this issue in life, we must admit when we are wrong. Are you able to do this to become victorious in an area that may have captured you?

A way you can achieve victory is to pray by faith that God will forgive your sin and empower your obedience. Admit you have sinned to whomever you have offended. Say you are sorry for the pain you have brought to God and others around you. Ask God for forgiveness and ask Him to wash all the prideful moments away. Ask God to give you strength by His Spirit, empowering you to no longer sin in pride, and then move to live in humility. As you pray this in Jesus' name, He will help you seek reconciliation and restitution where it is appropriate.

A word of caution - the devil will try to pull you back into your sin of pride. But continue in faith, being confident that God can transform your thinking.

Come into agreement with Him about the importance of humility in your life. Remind yourself that God is the One who deserves honor - not you. The power of God is more than enough to defend you against the spiritual tax of prideful behaviors.

> *In the same way, the younger ones should willingly support the leadership of the elders. In every relationship, each of you must wrap around yourself the apron of a humble servant. Because: God resists you when you are proud but multiplies grace and favor when you are humble.* (1 Peter 5:5 TPT)

ANGELA KAYE

is a child of God who was born in Jacksonville, Florida. With roots in Florida and Georgia, she has lived in Port Saint Lucie, Florida, for the past fifteen years.

Angela and her husband, Raul, have been married 18 years and have four children between them. Recognizing the hard work that marriage takes, they are intentional about putting God first and focusing on completing each other rather than competing with each other. Angela and Raul own their own painting business and love beautifying homes together. They also share a love for animals, especially dogs (having adopted many), gathering with other church families, volunteering at church, and helping others.

Angela aspires to be an active follower of God's Word, encourage others, and be truthful in all things. Although her life was once filled with many walls, by the grace of God, those walls are now removed, and she is living in Christ, learning to be quick to forgive and intentional with her actions for Christ.

FROM A WORRIER TO A WARRIOR!

BASED ON A MUSTARD SEED OF FAITH

By Angela Kaye

All my life, I have been a believer in the Father, Son, and Holy Spirit. My problem was that I was not a believer who was following Christ. I was not walking with Him in my daily life, moment by moment. I was not filled with scripture or sermons; instead I was filled by the world and living in reaction to it.

I did not understand the evils of this world, and I did not know how to fight using the armor of God. As God led me and I began to embrace the journey that He had me on, the sixth chapter in Ephesians became crucial to my life. I learned how to clothe myself in God's armor every day.

Growing up, I believed that success equaled a problem-free life, especially if you were a "good Christian." I did not know, as Ephesians 6:12 tells us, that I am not to fight against flesh and blood enemies, but against evil rulers and authorities of the unseen world, against mighty powers of the dark world, and against evil spirits in the heavenly places.

The women in my past have been worriers instead of warriors. And I followed in their path. As a child, I always had deep-seated fear and trust issues. I hid from visitors, including extended family. If we went out, I stayed attached to a parent if I could. As an adult, my fear and inability to trust nearly cost me my life. I knew I was to trust God, but I did not know how. And I didn't know the Bible could teach me.

I grew up in a Christian household; we did not attend church regularly, however. My mother was a true believer and always preached to us from Matthew 17:20 NIV: *He (Jesus) replied, "Because you have so little faith. Truly I tell you, if you have faith as small as a mustard seed, you can say to this mountain, 'Move from here to there,' and it will move. Nothing will be impossible for you."* She also liked to tell us anything was possible with Jesus in our hearts. She liked to pray and share her love for Jesus. She was my rock. Looking back, my mom's strength and wisdom had been hard-earned.

My mom suffered a lot of pain that stemmed from her childhood. When she was only sixteen, she lost her mother to cancer, who was only 44. Her mom was a believer who did not smoke or drink. The story goes that my grandmother died holding her Bible. My grandfather was a harsh man who let my mom know there was no place for her in his home after she graduated. I believe my parents married before they were ready because of this. Their marriage did not last.

My parents divorced when I was six and my sister was nine. They had been together for ten years. My mother left because of infidelity, though my father always denied this. My mother had her heart broken by my dad, and she wanted her daughters to never suffer that pain. She tried to protect us by teaching us to never count on anyone but ourselves. She instilled in us that we should only count on ourselves because everyone else would hurt us, including our mate and our father. So, I grew up fearing people, unable to form relationships. I saw my mom accomplish life alone successfully. Yet, I also dreamed of having a successful family life. I was just not sure what that looked like.

My mother did not remarry for twelve years after the divorce, when I was eighteen, so my sister and I were raised mainly in a single-parent household. As we grew up, she taught us stability and loyalty through her actions. She worked hard to give my sister and me things she did not have when growing up. She also wanted to prevent us from ever having our hearts broken, so she tried to shelter us as much as possible from the evils of the world. Her protection was out of love. As a little girl turning into an adult, I built many walls I was unaware I was building. I did not learn how to have relationships, or even the importance of relationships, but received warnings instead. I tried not to fear people, but I did, knowing that eventually, people would hurt me.

After my parents' divorce, my father married and divorced three more times. His second marriage also lasted ten years, which hurt as I saw him move on with a new family. He had three more daughters from that marriage. He was a great weekend daddy, and I always knew that he loved us, but that was not good enough – because he left us. He eventually left his second family, too. Technically, his second wife left him, but in my eyes, as a little girl, I just saw that he left them too. He always remained present in his girls' lives even though he did not raise any of us.

My dad always wanted a boy but did not get one, so he would comment to people that was the closest thing he ever got to a boy, and that would make me proud. He did his best to connect with us, even trying to make us proficient at vehicle maintenance, trying to make sure we were never taken advantage of when it came to cars. He loved cars.

I always seemed to be scared, but to make my dad proud, I pushed down my fear and became a "tomboy."

And to please my mom, I would try to stuff my fears down and be strong – tough and independent.

I bore the scars of being a child from a broken home who was trying to please her parents.

When I was 15 years old, I fell in "trust" instead of "love," and I married the first person I ever trusted when I was 20. The problem was we were not compatible as life partners. – I did not really know what love was because I had not seen a marriage work up close, and I especially did not understand God's love for me yet. We went through catholic marriage prep classes and a weekend retreat where we had our first and worst arguments ever. However, we were stubborn and ignored the signs and married anyway. We had a beautiful daughter, but our marriage only lasted for five years.

My daughter was two when we divorced. Unfortunately, our divorce was not amicable, and we fought over her most of her life. My ex-husband's parents were very involved in his fight against me. I had once been very close to this family, and the fact that they began fighting against me proved my mom's theory of people hurting you.

They wanted me out of my daughter's life, and I could not, nor did I want to, let go of my precious daughter. I only knew to fight for her, and my mom helped me. I began to feel the battles of life were never-ending, and I lost hope in humanity. I began down a very dark road I stayed on for a while, searching for value and love. Especially self-worth and self-love. I was alone and unable to trust people.

Eventually, I fell into an awful relationship which ended with me five months pregnant and in an emergency room from this man. I reassessed my life and sent my daughter to live with her dad, who resided with his parents after we divorced until they passed. I went to my father's home and regrouped until I had my second precious daughter. Both my daughters are miracles. Each has her own story. I am very proud of my girls.

My life was a mess, but I pulled it back together. I was still believing and thanking God for my blessings, but I was losing faith, and I began to live for my children. I did remarry. We were blessed with one of the most magnificent sunsets ever as we said our vows with dolphins jumping behind us. My new husband, Raul, and I were not putting God first, and life became one fire after another. We were both believers but not walking with Christ. Thankfully, our gracious God was pulling us to Him. We attended several different churches before we found our church home. However, by this time, my girls were older and decided they did not want to go to church with us, but they did come for special occasions, like my baptism, which was awesome.

The more I grew in my spiritual walk, the more the enemy came for me. And I did not know how to fight with the Word. I did not know what I did not know! My confidence was lacking, in fact, my confidence had dropped to zero. Raul and I began fighting more than talking. Returning to my childhood default, I became fearful all the time. I was hurt and full of anger. I used this anger to fuel me to fight. My girls were growing up with an angry, fearful mom. I was now carrying shame and guilt for not having lived for the Lord, but having lived for myself. I was learning Scripture which taught me who I am in Christ, but I was still struggling with not being good enough. I had feelings of shame because it had taken me so long to begin attending church, leading to the fact that I missed the opportunity to share church with my children. The "what if's" started to creep into my head. My husband and children were not going to church with me, and I wasn't even sure they had the same beliefs I did. This broke my heart. I was a failure. Even though I had put both my girls to bed with prayers as toddlers and they had great church experiences in their younger days, I had never found them a church home where they could find the spiritual support they needed outside the family. I've always believed in God, however I did not believe I was significant to God.. And, I knew the Lord was much smarter than me; He knew things that I could not possibly understand. I did not question God, but the flip side was that I did not grow in Him. I did not embrace the journey. Although I now had a church home that I attended regularly and even volunteered at, I was still not forming relationships. I did not know how. I had too many walls built up in my life.

I was under the misconception that when I accepted Jesus Christ as my Savior, somehow, everything was magically going to be okay. Well, it was not! It was getting more and more difficult, and I began to lose faith again. This time the devil stepped in powerfully. I was struggling in many areas of my life, and the devil began attacking me in all areas. Looking back, I know that I let him in through my doubt. But at my lowest point on my knees, I cried out for Jesus to forgive me. I was in my early fifties, struggling terribly through menopause, experiencing severe mood swings and deep depression. By this time, my children had both moved out, and my dear faithful mother had passed away at the age of 68 from early-onset Alzheimer's. I grew very close to my close friend Martha, who became a replacement for my mom, until she too passed away five years later. I did not know how to live without this support, and I could not find work after spending over three years caring for my mom, stepfather, and mother-in-law. With this, I lost more of my value. I felt like a failure as a mother, and my marriage of fifteen years was in turmoil. My life was essentially ending as I knew it. Everything was going to change; I was going to have to sell my home. I was broken. I was facing starting over with what felt like nothing. I could not even be proud of being a mother anymore, which was my most proud accomplishment.

The worst part was it sure seemed like God was not hearing my prayers. I felt I had been given more than I could bear. I decided to end my life July 7, 2018. I felt like the love I had given only hurt the ones I loved. I decided everyone I loved would be better off without me, especially financially, which seemed to always be a problem for us. I believed I would burn in hell, but decided I would rather burn than hurt them anymore. So, I decided to take some medication I had kept from my stepfather after he passed away. He was a man over 300 pounds and had two bottles of oxycodone and one bottle of Xanax. I easily took over seventy pills, and disposed of the packaging in the bottom of the trash so no one would know what I had taken. I locked my bedroom door and moved my dresser in front of the door so no one, not even my husband, could get in.

I then laid down and proceeded to pour my crazy emotions out on paper to my children and my husband. I was devastated by my husband, hurt and angry. I then prayed to God to please forgive me for what I had done. I begged and pleaded. And then I went to sleep.

My husband came home against everyone's advice to stay put and heard me mumbling. He had no idea of what I had taken. I had previously been on a mild anti-anxiety medication, and he thought maybe I had taken too much of that and would eventually sleep it off. But he stayed and heard what sounded like gurgling, so he began to try to enter the bedroom. This process, he said, took him about thirty minutes. He called 911, and the rescue to save my life began. I was given Narcan. I went into ICU and then mandatory rehabilitation. I came home July 25, 2018.

To this day, I regret the letters I wrote, and I have no recollection of what I wrote, except that they were hurtful. Nor did I hear Raul pour his heart out to me while I was unconscious. Miraculously, my recovery was immediate from the time I awoke. My mustard seed of faith, at my lowest point, had saved my life. Now, I know I am a child of God worth saving and that I have purpose versus a purpose. I have watched people leave in my life, so I learned to leave. I was not sure of how to stay. Now, I am learning to give my troubles to the Lord. I am learning to be still and trust in the Lord.

From a Worrier to a Warrior! Based on
a Mustard Seed of Faith - Angela Kaye

243

Raul and I now put God first, and our lives have made a complete turnaround. Although our children are not pursuing a life for Christ currently, I've learned to give this to our Father and pray for their souls. With God all things are possible, even with just a mustard seed of faith.

I know more troubles and obstacles are coming, but today I fight my worries with prayer. I am a prayer warrior, and I encourage you, no matter where you are on your journey, to join me. Through prayer, God has given me a renewed peace. I'm able to experience more joy and goodwill as I humbly, as a sinner, receive in God's grace. I start my day in prayer with my husband; I also pray with my best friend and intercede on behalf of many. And, of course, I pray by myself.

I also continue to learn Scripture through sermons, and group studies. I continue to thrive as I learn more on this journey with Christ. It can only get better with God. I have found that the more I learn, the more God had to teach me. The Bible is our guide, and we must know what's in it.

I've also learned the value of Christian fellowship. God has taught me that we learn in fellowship with other like-minded followers in small groups. I look forward to communion with others in godly friendships I have begun to build. Yes, there are people who will hurt you, but when you give the control to God, you can trust that He will see you through even the times of hurt and pain.

I encourage anyone who is not walking with Christ in their daily life to start by giving Him the first fifteen minutes of your day. Five minutes in prayer, five minutes in worship, and five minutes in Scripture. Embracing this small change daily has improved my life tremendously. I now have a renewed confidence because I saw the footprints in the sand story come to life as He carried me. I still struggle, but now I can pray about it and be led back to the Word by my church family, who encourages me and quotes Scripture over my life. I can breathe better down deep in my soul now. I'm proud to say my true family rallied behind me, and I am on the best path in life I have ever been on.

Please know with all your heart what I have learned: you can trust in our Father, and become a warrior rather than a worrier. I am thankful for another chance at life, knowing I have God to carry me when I cannot carry myself. I can suit up with the armor of God as described in Ephesians 6, and fight for my God.

Stand firm then, with the belt of truth buckled around your waist, with the breastplate of righteousness in place, and with your feet fitted with the readiness that comes from the gospel of peace. In addition to all this, take up the shield of faith, with which you can extinguish all the flaming arrows of the evil one. Take the helmet of salvation and the sword of the Spirit, which is the word of God.

And pray in the Spirit on all occasions with all kinds of prayers and requests. With this in mind, be alert and always keep on praying for all the Lord's people. (Ephesians 6:14-18, NIV)

CONQUERING VANITY

by Julie T. Jenkins

Vanity is excessive pride in our appearance or achievements. Someone who is vain thinks a lot of herself and thinks about herself a lot. Interestingly, the Latin origins of the word *vanus* means empty or without substance. Now isn't that just the last thing that a vain person would want to be considered – empty and without substance?

Proverbs 31 introduces us to a woman who is the opposite of vain, whose life is full as she goes about her day focused on others. In the NIV, this woman is described as "a wife of noble character" (v 10) who, through her actions, is a blessing to others. She "works with eager hands" (v 13), "provides food for her family" (v 15) and makes sure her they are kept warm (v 21-22). In addition to taking care of her family, she "sets about her work vigorously" (v 17) as she makes certain her lamp stays lit (v 18), "extends her hands to the needy" (v 20), and conducts business in her community (v 24).

This woman thinks more about who she is and how she can keep a positive attitude than about how she looks or what she has accomplished. "She is clothed with strength and dignity; she can laugh at the days to come." (v 25)

She thinks about how she can affect others. "She speaks with wisdom, and faithful instruction is on her tongue." (v 26)

She cares about her family and pushes through even the tough days rather than resting on her laurels. "She watches over the affairs of her household and does not eat the bread of idleness." (v 27)

She realizes that substance is worth so much more than outward appearances. "Charm is deceptive and beauty is fleeting." (v 30)

Most importantly, she realizes what is most important – the Lord Himself. She takes the focus off herself and puts it on the Lord. "...a woman who fears the Lord is to be praised." (v 30)

Vanity. This overt focus on our looks and pride in our achievements is fleeting, which, like flowers in a vase, will wilt, fade, and die - leaving nothing but dust and residue.

In contrast, our actions and love for others will bloom again and again, like a flower planted in good soil. Although the seasons will change and force the seeds to blow in the wind, those seeds will find fertile ground in the upcoming season, and the woman's legacy will live on.

How do we conquer vanity? By focusing our gaze on God's everlasting purpose for our lives. No matter how beautiful we are outwardly, our true beauty comes only from God and His hand on our lives. May our prayer always be Psalm 119:35-37 (NIV)...

> *Direct me in the path of your commands,*
> *for there I find delight.*
> *Turn my heart toward your statutes*
> *and not toward selfish gain.*
> *Turn my eyes away from worthless things;*
> *preserve my life according to your word.*

· ·

AFTERWORD

As you step out in faith each day that you live, keep standing your ground, decreeing your victory no matter what you see right now. There will be sudden displays of the triumph of Jesus in your life as you follow Him in obedience. You can count on it. As you've read this book, the authors have prayed for you. They have prayed that cages of limitations will be opened in life, while identity issues, fear, intimidation, depression, anxiety, and strongholds will suddenly become contained. We have prayed you will break free from any captivity that once enslaved you from having true victory in Jesus and that you will be propelled into newfound freedom in Christ.

We hope you have encountered God's heart as you've read these stories of women claiming victory from secret places that God led them through. May your own garden of hidden privacy be awakened to see the beauty of God, and may you trust Him if He calls you to share your battle to help another. Remember the scripture shared at the beginning of this book, Revelation 12:11, "And they overcame him by the blood of the Lamb, and by the word of their testimony." (KJV)

Yes, God is awakening warriors within the body of Christ to step up and be heard as they live with boldness and courage as overcomers in Christ Jesus. Then and only then will there be the freedom in Christ and the power of God released to defeat the enemy. What do you have to look forward to as God's warrior? For one, the devil will be reminded through you over and over that victory is in Jesus; and secondly, he will be reminded that he has been conquered by Christ's death on the cross and His resurrection. May you trust God through the saving blood of Jesus Christ and seek Him by faith for your victory in life.

Arise, Jerusalem! Let your light shine for all to see. For the glory of the Lord rises to shine on you. (Isaiah 60:1 NLT)